Beyond Dying

D0589233

Beyond DYING

THE MYSTERY OF ETERNITY

TED HARRISON

A LION BOOK

Copyright © 2000 Ted Harrison

The author asserts the moral right
to be identified as the author of this work

Published by
Lion Publishing plc
Sandy Lane West, Oxford, England
www.lion-publishing.co.uk
ISBN 0 7459 5047 7

First hardback edition 2000
First paperback edition 2001
10 9 8 7 6 5 4 3 2 1 0

A catalogue record for this book is available
from the British Library

Printed and bound in Great Britain by
Omnia Books Limited, Glasgow

Contents

INTRODUCTION 7

CHAPTER ONE: *An Ancient Mystery* 14

CHAPTER TWO: *Death of the Body* 28

CHAPTER THREE: *Forbidden Knowledge?* 52

CHAPTER FOUR: *Where is the Evidence?* 78

CHAPTER FIVE: *Scripture and Tradition* 107

CHAPTER SIX: *The Good News* 125

CHAPTER SEVEN: *Looking Death in the Face* 139

CHAPTER EIGHT: *Preparing, Planning and Thwarting* 157

CHAPTER NINE: *We Will All Go Together, When We Go* 168

CHAPTER TEN: *Graves and Grieving* 174

CHAPTER ELEVEN: *Public Mourning* 186

CHAPTER TWELVE: *The Insight of Children* 196

EPILOGUE: *The Mystery of Transcendence* 203

NOTES 213

ACKNOWLEDGMENTS 221

Introduction

Anyone who, like me, has reached middle-age will almost undoubtedly have had some sort of brush with death. It may have been in the form of an accident, an attack, a close shave in a car or an illness. Whatever form it took it would have served as a reminder of human, and one's own, mortality. In my own case it was kidney disease that provided the salutary lesson:

As 1985 progressed I began to feel increasingly tired yet unable to relax. My legs twitched as an unbearable tension built up. I found my concentration waning and by June I must have been very ill... and found I could not work for more than half an hour at a time. Much of the day was spent lying down or sitting in the round greenhouse in the garden which trapped the northern sun...

I do not now recall how long I was in hospital. Days seem to merge into each other in my memory. I recall the endless sleepless nights when I could not lie still for more than a minute or two at a time and had to walk the corridor to get any respite from the muscular tensions caused by the poisons in my body...

In short bursts I would work on my book...

Despite wrestling with matters theological in the course of my writing I felt too ill to have many deep thoughts of my own. If I had died then it would have been a strange anticlimax to life. After a week or two in hospital all passion and hope had left me and I just survived.[1]

Had I been born even ten years earlier, or been born in a different country, or class, without access to modern medicine, I would not be alive today. Twenty years ago I was diagnosed as having progressive kidney failure and, as described above, in an account written three years after the events, in the days before I was started on kidney dialysis I was very close to dying. A few days or weeks more and my poisoned blood would not have been able to sustain me and life would have petered out – that is, if a potassium overload had not felled me with a heart attack sooner. Fortunately I survived, but that close encounter with death gave me good reason to pause for thought.

There are some people who spend their lives with the dying; I am not one of them. I am no Mother Teresa or Dame Cicely Saunders.[2] Neither am I an undertaker, hospice worker, paramedic or pathologist dealing with death on a daily basis. I am typical of my generation in that I have seen few corpses and only twice have I witnessed a person's dying moments. So my view of life is not, as it must be with the professionals who regularly deal with death and its consequences, overloaded with images of death.

If I have one qualification to write about the subject of death it is that I have perhaps gone just a little beyond the standard brush with death. I could say that I have been, if not through death's door, at least standing on the doorstep. To which I would add a second qualification: I owe my continued existence in good health to the death of someone else – not someone I ever met. I call him or her – I do not know the gender – the friend I never knew. I refer to the donor of the transplanted kidney I was given and which for over nine years has sustained me. Looked at dispassionately, it may be seen as both an irony and a profundity of life that I have enjoyed an extension to my time on earth due to the fact that someone else's life was cut short. It has given me an unusual and challenging perspective on death, especially as I have had to assimilate into my life a range of feelings and emotions associated with the circumstance of the transplant. The donor, I can reasonably assume, did not want or expect to die. Logically I know that

I was not the cause of the donor's death. Yet I cannot help but recall how, when I was suffering from kidney failure and undergoing regular haemodialysis, a kidney transplant was what I desperately wanted. Thus to feel entirely free of responsibility for the donor's death is difficult. I did not wish death upon anyone, but nevertheless I hoped that should someone die, I would be the beneficiary.

I have had good reason, therefore, to think about death. Not, I hope, in any morbid obsessive sense, but in a constructive way. I am fortunate in that my view has not been obscured by the tears of untimely grief. Those of my family who have died have done so naturally and, in most cases, in the fullness of time. Consequently I feel that in writing about death I can be both informed by experience and objective in outlook.

There are as many ways of dying as there are individual people. Each death is a unique experience. Nevertheless death can be divided into two types: natural and traumatic. The majority of people die naturally. They reach old age or contract a naturally occurring illness, which takes them step by step towards death's door with the final moment coming suddenly, as with a heart attack, or in a slower, peaceful and more prepared way. The minority die traumatically in accidents or wars, as victims, or in a host of other ways which cut short a life before its natural conclusion.

Within both of these categories there are special factors to be borne in mind when an infant dies, either before or after birth, before having had a chance to experience life. A stillbirth, a cot death, the death of a toddler from disease – whatever the cause and whatever the age of the child, his or her death can be especially sorrowful. Parents often find irrational reasons to blame themselves, particularly when a death is the result of an avoidable accident. Guilt and grief can be interwoven.

It can be argued that we live in an increasingly safety-conscious world. Manufacturers are obliged to ensure that children's toys contain no hidden dangers. None of the classic children's toys of a century ago would pass today's safety inspections. Lead soldiers or dainty dolls' house knick-knacks might be swallowed. Clockwork trains have sharp metal edges and might cut a child's fingers. Children today are not generally allowed the freedom to roam the streets or the countryside, although their parents or grandparents took this for granted. The perceived dangers are such – whether in the form of road traffic or strangers with dubious motives – that few children are even allowed to walk to school and are ferried backwards and forwards in the family car.

When risk is eliminated from so many aspects of life, children learn that anything uncertain and unknown is to be feared. Many become timid. Confined to the safety of the home, children today learn about death second- and third-hand from the television. They do not learn the facts of death in the course of learning the facts of life. I remember how, when I was young in the late fifties and early sixties, I would find dead birds and animals as I roamed the countryside, with my friends, unsupervised. I would look at their stiff corpses, touch them, smell them and marvel at their delicate structures. I would wonder how the life-force had vanished from them. There were times, too, as a small boy, when I killed creepy-crawlies of various kinds and learned from the experience. There was a country market near to where I lived and when trading had finished on market day I would see the animals being taken by the drovers to the local butchers' shops. Later I would see the meat hanging in the shop windows. Some of the best cuts would have a coloured rosette pinned to them to show that the animal had, in life, won a prize at a cattle show. There was never a time when I did not know that the meat on my plate had come from a farm animal. Today many children have to be taught in school that the cling-film-wrapped sausage from the supermarket was made from part of a pig. For some the news comes both as a shock and a surprise. When they learn how few farm animals are reared in such a way that they enjoy a free and idyllic life and how many are destined for a brutal and stressful death, many of today's more sensitive children opt to become vegetarians.

Many contemporary young people remain protected even as they approach adulthood. The intrepid backpacking students, who set off to wander around the world on a great adventure before settling down to boring adult life, do their best to minimize risk. They keep a lifeline, the emergency money sewn into the lining of the jacket or the home telephone number to be contacted by the consul in case of an emergency.

Death, however, is a journey without a lifeline. It is a journey without a route map, and when we set out we have no idea where we are going. Sometimes a person embarks on it with no time to get ready; on other occasions a person may be given plenty of warning signs, but opt to ignore them all. Even those who do prepare themselves as best they can know that, when the hour of death arrives, they go out into the unknown alone.

Like the ancient nautical charts of old, on which unknown seas were marked with fearsome pictures of sea monsters and dragons to denote danger, so our mental picture of death is full of dire warnings. Is hell awaiting us, or purgatory, or oblivion? In death will we lose our bearings? Will everything familiar and reassuring be taken from us? No wonder that the most popular psalm, said or sung, at British funeral services is Psalm 23, 'The Lord is My Shepherd'. It gives hope that the journey is not taken alone: 'Yea, though I walk through the valley of the shadow of death, I will fear no evil: for thou art with me; thy rod and thy staff they comfort me.'[3]

In this book I will look at what is meant by death in the physical sense. Then I will examine the evidence as to what we will experience beyond the grave. That will be the main thrust of the work – starting with a résumé of the main types of belief in the afterlife and continuing with an analysis of the ideas and theories which have been floated as to what we can expect to find beyond our earthly and physical demise. There are dozens of clues to be had, but a lot of them are unhelpful. Even if 50 per cent of the supposed insights into the world beyond are true and 50 per cent are delusions, there is no way of telling which 50 per cent to believe.

I have spoken to many people about their own ideas of death and I have read widely. I have drawn on my own experiences and memories.

Not long ago my father died. He had reached a good age and his death was not unexpected, yet his final weeks were distressing for my mother and the family to watch as it seemed that the progressive deterioration of his senses and memory disorientated him. In his final weeks, following a stroke, he spent much of the time asleep, but when he woke, he appeared to find the hospital ward around him unfamiliar, and he seemed to become increasingly anxious about losing control of his failing body.

Gradually, working through all of this – memories, experiences and research findings – while I still find so many questions about death to be as mysterious as ever, I have reached a position from where it is possible to accept mystery. And in accepting mystery it is often possible to shed fear. I have even become excited by the possibilities of what might be to come. As fascinating and amazing as this world is, what greater and more awesome reality might lie beyond?

I have discovered, too, that I am not alone in formulating certain ideas. Writers like Elisabeth Kübler-Ross and Kathleen Dowling Singh have cut paths ahead of me through the jungle of conjecture. Kübler-Ross took a psychoanalytical and psychospiritual approach.[5] Singh set out from the same place, but followed a more mystical path.[6] She has written of the grace of dying and how we are transformed spiritually as we die.

As important as this type of pioneering work has been – and I make no claims to match it in depth or perception – there are many people who would like to follow it, but who get lost on the way. This book, I hope, is for the growing army of stragglers, lost in the confusion of the subject, who want to learn as much as they can about that journey which they are destined one day to take. We, of this present generation, are not the first to want to understand death. It is, and has always been, part of the human condition to revere and fear death and at the same time to ask questions about it. As far as we know, as humans we are unique among animals in that we bury, or otherwise dispose of, our dead with care and ceremony. And often it is by studying the ways different cultures perform, or have performed, this function, that we discover the fascinating peoples and communities of our fellow human beings. From time immemorial it seems different peoples and traditions have attempted to discern the nature of God through death.

It is difficult for any of us, when fit and active and full of the joys of life, to think about our own death. It is something for which we are not psychologically suited. We can become quickly frightened, or overawed, by the questions we ask. Might death be a permanent state of nothingness without form or awareness? Will it be entirely different from anything else we have experienced or prepared ourselves for? Will there truly be heaven? From time to time we might ask ourselves these things, but usually they are far from our mind as we concentrate on day-to-day living.

'As with every other looming terror and looming temptation,' wrote Dr Sherwin Nuland, 'we seek ways to deny the power of death and the icy hold in which it grips human thought. Its constant closeness has always inspired traditional methods by which we consciously or unconsciously disguise its reality, such as folk tales, allegories, dreams and even jokes.'[7]

In recent times, Dr Nuland suggests, the developed Western world has created a new way to disguise that reality – the method of modern dying. Modern dying takes place in the modern hospital, where it can be hidden, cleansed of its organic blight, and finally packaged for modern burial.

The classic deathbed scene, it was observed forty years ago, 'with its loving partings and solemn last words, is practically a thing of the past; in its stead is a sedated, comatose, betubed object, manipulated and subconscious, if not subhuman'.[8] 'We can deny the power not only of death but of nature itself,' Dr Nuland observed. 'We hide our faces from its face.'[9] And yet death draws us to itself. It is ultimately irresistible. As we hide our faces like children, thinking that what we cannot see cannot see us, 'we still spread our fingers just a bit, because there is something in us that cannot resist a peek'.[10]

CHAPTER ONE

An Ancient Mystery

The noon sun was shining from a clear blue sky. The receding tide had revealed a beach of white sand. A light, but chill breeze was blowing off the sea. Twenty yards from the shore a seal surfaced, raised its head and watched. At the high-tide mark a funeral pyre had been prepared, as yet unlit and cold.

A small group of people, some thirty in number, had gathered at the scene. Three men approached the pyre carrying a bier made from two wooden poles laced together with twine. On it lay a corpse for cremation. The place of cremation had been marked off from the rest of the beach by a circle of stones placed in the sand. The men carrying the bier entered the circle by walking between two lines of stones placed like an avenue at the entrance. They laid their burden gently on the neat stack of wood and peat and stepped back.

A few moments passed and they withdrew further to where there was a small pile of grey and white heated peat, glowing red from within. It was in a shallow depression hollowed out of the sand to protect it from the wind. From this, their fire store, they took some smouldering bricks on a small spade. They placed the live peats, which had been carefully prepared and kept alight for the occasion, inside the pyre at one end. They returned to the source of the fire and took more live peats and placed them beneath the corpse at the other end. They then retreated and stood back with the others who had gathered to watch.

It took several minutes for smoke to appear and almost half an hour passed before the stacked dry wood and peat of the pyre began to burn. Satisfied that the fire had taken hold, the people slowly left the scene – a few returning from time to time to see that the fire stayed alight. Twenty-four hours later the fire had burned itself out and had rendered the corpse to ash. When the ashes were cool they were carefully gathered.

In August 1999 I was in Shetland when I heard that a team of archaeologists was planning to simulate a Bronze Age human cremation. It was part of an ongoing project exploring the historic and prehistoric past of Britain's most northerly island community. As a frequent visitor to Shetland it seemed to me that to watch the simulation would be a fascinating opportunity to learn more about the history of the place. And so it was that on the day appointed, my wife and I and two friends went along to the beach at Sumburgh where the cremation was to take place.

The corpse selected for the purpose was not human, but that of an elderly (and humanely dispatched) sheep from a local farm. The funeral pyre was, however, as authentic as the team could make it. It was around five feet long, four feet high and three feet broad. The sides of the structure were made from poles of wood, each some three inches in diameter. The structure was then infilled with deep-brown-coloured peat, cut from the local hills and dried in the open air into fragile bricks, which could be crumbled between finger and thumb. The pyre itself was carefully positioned to face the prevailing wind of the day.

The purpose of the archaeologists' experiment, they explained, was to understand more about the science of cremation as carried out by the Shetlanders of 4,000 years ago. Human remains from burials of both earlier and later dates have been found in profusion in the Northern Isles, but evidence has also been unearthed which suggests that in the Bronze Age cremation, too, was a common way of disposing of human remains.

What the scientists and historians did not know was how, in a place where very little wood was available for fuel, the ancient people had managed to created the temperatures required for cremation using mainly peat as fuel. The answer, so the archaeologists surmised, lay in the design and construction of the funeral pyre. They knew that there had been a small supply of wood available at the time. Some of it would have been driftwood gathered from the beaches, and some of it would have been coppiced from the few areas of managed woodland on the islands. Bronze Age man and woman, it was conjectured, had shaped and used the wood to make a firm open structure into which blocks of the locally dried peat turf had been packed. The positioning of the structure had been particularly important, the scientists thought, to enable the wind to blow through it providing the oxygen for combustion.

The modern-day reconstruction using the remains of a sheep, peats, driftwood and locally coppiced staves proved that cremation was possible. If, indeed, the pyre had been a faithful recreation of a Bronze Age one, the experiment demonstrated that the people of the time clearly understood the techniques and the physics involved in disposing of human remains by fire.

While the scientists from the Shetland Amenity Trust and Bradford University were satisfied that they had found the technical answers to their questions, they admitted that their knowledge was incomplete. Their adviser, Jackie McKinley from Salisbury, an expert on the historical techniques of cremation, was ready to admit that she had no clear idea as to the context of cremation. It was not known what rituals would have surrounded the event, she told me. There was little way of knowing what the people of the time believed happened to the person whose mortal remains they destroyed by fire. To have deduced that from modern experimentation and examination of the archaeological record would have been impossible. There were, however, clues to be had and these had been carefully recorded from excavations. From studying the remains of cremations of the period it would appear that offerings were left next to the corpse on the funeral pyre. So it was that a reconstruction of a pot from the period was filled with milk and left by the sheep's head as part of the modern experiment.

Leaving gifts for the departed is not an uncommon practice. There are examples, from other times and places, of the graves of rich and important people being filled with such items, including horses and slaves slaughtered to accompany their owner or employer. The less wealthy had simpler gifts left in the ground beside them. The practice continues in the Western world today. In her booklet prepared to help families arrange a funeral, the 'agony aunt' Virginia Ironside writes of what people in Britain often do if they visit a funeral parlour to say their farewells to someone they love: 'Some people find it healing to see the person at rest and like to bring a little gift, or photograph, or piece of jewellery to put in the coffin. This will be buried with the body.'[1] As studies by modern social anthropologists have shown, when gifts are left, especially those which had a practical use in life, it is often evidence of a belief in an afterlife. If not that precisely, then it is evidence of rituals being practised which have meaning. It suggests that disposing of a corpse is seen by the survivors as more than just a utilitarian response to a death. If the deed is accompanied by ritual, that ritual may serve one of several purposes from which both mourners and the departed are believed to benefit.

If gifts of food were given to be cremated by the Bronze Age Shetlanders it might be implied that they believed the departed was journeying to another place. In the same way that a living person embarking on a journey would need provisions, so would the dead. But how would the deceased use these provisions in an afterlife if their earthly corpse was being turned to ash? The answer lies in the symbolism, and ritual is symbolism embodied in action. One can only suppose these things, but it seems likely that had a pot of milk been presented to the dead person on the pyre, it was as a gesture and expression of faith. Its presentation at the cremation strongly implies that in the culture of the time there existed some concept of the soul – that the essence of the dead person survived after death in a form which did not require an earthly body. As Professor Douglas Davies points out in his overview of contemporary funeral rites, 'Some idea of soul or spirit seems to have played an important part in helping many different societies to express their conviction that life does not end with physical death.'[2]

The idea of a soul is common to many cultures, but the exact definition of a soul and its purpose and attributes is not agreed. Some philosophers have suggested that the soul, or essential person, is the ability to think and be aware of self. Others suggest it involves an awareness of time or moral principle. There are also those who think that a soul might not be identified with an individual in perpetuity. They suggest that the ultimate destiny of the soul is to shed its separate identity and merge into a greater consciousness. There is no agreement either as to where the soul is located in life. Some people believe the soul is to be found in the heart, others say the liver or blood. We in the Western world, if pressed, might say the soul – or at least the personality as many would prefer to define it – is centred on the brain and its complex functions. In some cultures every animal is said to have a soul. Animists would regard all animals, plants and geological features as having or containing a spirit.

But from where do such ideas come? Is belief in a soul part of the collective consciousness of the human race, or does each separate culture discover the idea for itself in isolation? Or perhaps the notion of the soul is one that originated from a single source, but was passed from culture to culture as different tribal groups made contact with each other. There undoubtedly was contact between the scattered settlements of the sparsely inhabited prehistoric world. In some places artefacts have been found that could only have originated many miles away. We know that for millennia people have travelled. Indeed, long before the European Bronze Age great migrations of population took place. The forebears of the native Americans, for instance, are thought to have come across the Bering Strait from Asia on a now long-lost land link to settle a new continent. They share inherited characteristics with people of Asia that strongly imply a common ancestry. The most recent migration theories now suggest that these early American settlers themselves displaced other people living there who were genetically linked to the Aborigines of Australia. Transport in the pre-industrial age was slow, but using both land and sea routes was possible. How else would communities have become established in places like Shetland if navigation and seamanship were not practised?

We know that with travel there is trade, normally in both goods and ideas. We cannot, of course, know how far ideas would have travelled, but we do know some of the ideas that were prevalent in the world at the time of the Bronze Age Shetlanders, and that they contain within them the notion that the soul survives death. In the Middle East there were civilizations contemporary with the Bronze Age settlements of offshore Europe which had begun to record their thoughts and their deeds in writing. Thousands of clay tablets have been found from the archaeological remains of the towns and cities of Mesopotamia. These places were thriving and sophisticated civilizations 4,000 years ago. From these tablets there is ample evidence to be had of trade and travel.

The artefacts and buildings, some of quite astonishing proportions, associated with Egypt during the second and third millennia before Christ, also bear their own testimony. Around 2000 BC the palaces and towns of the Minoan civilization of Crete were being built and hieroglyphics were being used. At the same time in China the Shang civilization was emerging and in South America large-scale maize farming was being developed in the Peruvian Andes. And perhaps most vivid of all the records, there is the detailed account of the history of the Jewish people dating from this time and preserved in the Old Testament. What emerges from reading the books of Jewish law, history and poetry is far more than can be discovered from examining the debris of prehistory. There are insights into the loves, hates, feuds, jealousies, hopes and fears of an ancient people. Most important of all is the evidence of the relationship between the people of the past and their God.

The settlements of the Shetland Bronze Age people who practised cremation survived for many generations across several centuries. Their contemporaries quite possibly included the great names of the Old Testament. Traditional biblical chronology suggests that Abraham lived around 2000 BC, and Jacob, Joseph and Moses lived during the centuries that followed. It is interesting to reflect, in the context of the ancient Shetland people, on one of the best-known stories of the time that comes to us from the book of Genesis in the Old Testament. It tells how Abraham, when tested by God, builds a funeral pyre on which to sacrifice his son. Abraham collects wood, and takes fire to set it alight, to offer his son as sacrifice. (The story was later interpreted by Christians as anticipating the sacrifice of Christ.) Only at the very last minute does the angel of the Lord intervene. Abraham is told not to slay his son and as he looks up he sees a ram caught in a thicket. He kills the ram and offers it instead. The aim of the story is to tell how God tested Abraham's faith to the limit, but it is also a very early reference to the idea that death can have a purpose: Isaac was not, in the end, killed, but his father had been prepared to do the deed to demonstrate his complete confidence that God knew what was best. Consequently, he readied himself to kill his son and offer him as a burnt sacrifice.[3]

Abraham himself died an old man. He was not cremated but buried in the cave of Machpelah. The place is carefully identified by the Genesis writer. And, as if to emphasize how peoples living hundreds of miles apart shared many of the same cultural practices, there have been numerous finds of burials in cave-like chambers in the Northern Isles. Some of these chambers have been excavated in modern times and are open to visitors. They are like large vaults, and they contained the remains of several individuals in their own defined space or chambers. The island of Rousay in Orkney, to the south of Shetland, has some of the best-preserved examples at Midhowe and Blackhammer. They have been described as elaborately constructed houses for the dead and were not unlike the houses in which the living sheltered. These great cairns would have taken many months to construct and their existence implies that the disposal of human remains was not a task to be taken lightly. Huge slabs of stone had to be quarried and transported. Much human strength and cooperation would have been involved and it would, therefore, have been a community activity. The nature of burials such as these suggests they were more than simply a practical way of getting rid of the remains of a corpse. It implies that the people of the period believed that the elaborate disposal of the dead which they practised had an important symbolic purpose.

Much of what we know about the prehistoric islanders of the north has been learned from a close examination of the burial remains. It is possible to deduce from the bones and teeth a range of information about life in those distant days. From each skeleton the specialists in various fields of expertise can determine gender, age, diet and state of health of any individual disintered. Even the cause of death can often be found.

At the time of the Bronze Age cremations, the Northern Isles of Britain already had a long history of habitation. At the Knap of Howar on the island of Papa Westray in Orkney, houses were excavated which have been dated to between 3600 and 3100 BC. Famously, an entire village made of stone survives at Skara Brae, inhabited 1,000 years before the Bronze Age. There it is possible to discern beds, cupboards and hearths made out of slabs of local stone. An examination of the rubbish left behind on the site gives some idea as to how the people survived. They caught fish from the sea and lochs and gathered shellfish from the shore. Cattle, pigs, sheep and goats were reared and barley was sown and harvested. They collected the eggs of seabirds. They had pottery, which they made in a style later identified by characteristic grooved decorative marks. As archaeologist Anna Ritchie points out, evidence of not only day-to-day living, but also that of art and decoration was discovered at Skara Brae. This unearthing of pattern and design suggests that the people of 5,000 years ago were not solely concerned with survival. They looked beyond the material world and sought beauty as well as utility in their possessions. As Ritchie wrote,

> There is a remarkable number of decorated stones from Skara Brae. The motifs are mostly based on chevrons, triangles, zig-zags, executed by incised lines... Most of the decoration was carved on passage walls, and only two houses were decorated internally... and the ornaments may have had a special significance... If decoration carried special meaning other than a pleasure in its existence, the key is hidden.[4]

But what did the peoples, surviving for several millennia in the harsh conditions of the Northern Isles, make of their world? Did they speculate about its purpose and origin? Living in a place where the forces of nature – the power of wind and the sea and the cycles of the year – are ever present, one can imagine they held those forces in respect and awe. Did they identify them with divine forces? Did they believe that a God revealed himself to them and protected them, as Jehovah spoke to and through the prophets of Israel? Was the God they knew seen as the vengeful God of storm and famine, or the loving God of good harvest and celebration? We do not know, but again clues have been left behind that perhaps they conceived of God as a duality, and these will be mentioned later on in this book.

In several modern-day belief systems, nature is believed to consist of two opposed but mutually dependent parts – the male and the female. Pre-Christian cultures in Europe are believed to have identified the sun as representing the male and the moon as representing the female.

Anna Ritchie drew attention to the arrangement of furniture at Skara Brae, which suggested that items for female use were kept to the left and those for male use kept to the right. 'It may suggest', she wrote, 'that one view of the world held by the inhabitants concerned duality, a very common feature of human cosmology.'[5]

George Terence Meaden believes a clue may be found in the pottery decoration. He claims that the symbolism is consistent with that found throughout what he describes as 'the Goddess-worshipping societies from Stonehenge to Orkney'.[6] His work is speculative, despite its claim to have found the secret of Stonehenge, but has a plausibility to it. He describes a time when Britain was inhabited by people who followed a peaceful, nature-loving religion which ruled the lives of the early farming communities before their way of life was overturned by warrior tribes. As these ancient people depended upon the tilling of the fields and the harvesting of the crops for their food, so the farming process depended upon the cycles of the year. Meaden and others suggest that their myths explained the cycles in terms of the bonding of the male and female aspects of the deity. Their divine fertility ensured the fertility of the soil. Built into this view of the world is an acceptance of death. In autumn, plants are seen to wither and die in preparation for the sleep of winter and rebirth in the spring. Death is thus seen as the end of the season of growth, but at the same time a prerequisite of birth.

To accept the possibility that there once existed a group of people who worshipped the female aspects of a deity so many thousands of years ago is to gain a tantalizing insight into the possible thinking of the people of a remote age. Yet to give the picture of life and belief in those distant times substance and colour, one perhaps has to rely on more than the evidence taken from the scientific analysis of soil and remnants, however well informed. One has to draw on a knowledge of human nature and transpose it in time and space.

To the modern onlookers watching the simulated human cremation on the beach in Shetland, and peering through the smoke of the pyre to the sea, the rocks and the horizon, nothing impinged on the line of sight which could not have been there in those distant prehistoric times. It was the perfect visual backdrop against which to imagine a scene from 4,000 years ago. The aroma of the burning peat added an additional sensory dimension. The smoke and the smell of the sea was much as it would have been all those years ago. Only the sounds of the world around would have been substantially different, for the beach was close to the island's airport, and aircraft movements and the noise of motor traffic impinged on the sounds of the natural and primitive world. To complete an authentic impression of Bronze Age times, the imagination needed to block out the extraneous sounds and fill in the extra details.

Four thousand years earlier, at a real cremation of a member of the tribe, there would undoubtedly have been mourners weeping. They might have been dressed or painted to express their grief. Would there have been an elder, shaman or priest dressed in animal skins with face and head covered in a decorated mask, performing rituals? He would have been there, or so the people believed, to release the soul from the body and speed the departed on his or her journey to the other world. There might have been music, the beating of a skin drum, the wailing of a hand-carved bone pipe, singing and chanting. The shaman would have known about the naturally occurring hallucinogens and used them, together with the musical rhythms, to give himself an illusion of transcendence in order, so he might have believed, to pilot and guide the soul of the departed to another world.

One can imagine, too, a grieving mother; a spouse left behind; children barely able to understand what the loss of a parent meant. Who was the person they mourned? How had he or she died? Had there been an accident? Had there been disease? Had there been war or murder or suicide? What had been done to the corpse before cremation? Had it been reverently dressed and anointed? What was to happen to the ashes after cremation? Were they to be scattered to the winds, or would the site, now consecrated by the ritual, have been left or covered over?

The language spoken by the people, the symbolism of the rituals, the clothes and decorations worn by those gathered around the pyre, would all appear strange to us today. However, the emotions felt and expressed by the family and friends would have been those which are universal to the human condition. Modern men and women would instantly empathize; grief is an emotion which crosses all cultural boundaries. On television news clips, the grieving mothers of young men lost in war in Africa appear, in their displays of their distraught selves, little different from the grieving mothers of children lost in natural disasters in, say, South America. From Aberfan to Northern Ireland to Kosovo to Rwanda to East Timor to Turkey, tragedy produces an identical response – as it has done throughout history.

Four thousand years ago, all over the inhabited world, there would have been rituals and practices to mark the departure from life in this world to life in the next world, a place beyond the reach of human knowledge. The rituals would have had two purposes: firstly, to appease the unknown forces of death, allowing the dead a trouble-free passage to the next world, and secondly, to provide a safe and accepting context within which mourners felt free to express their deepest feelings. But however extravagant or simple the rites – and these often depended upon the status of the dead person – the bottom-line reality would have been the same. In death, the pharaoh in Egypt, embalmed and laid in a sumptuous tomb, would be have been as equally at the mercy of the unknown as the dead Shetland child, mother or warrior.

To all generations, and in all cultures, death brings with it the same mix of fear and hope. Going to a funeral, whatever form it takes, is a reminder of our own mortality. It is a chance to say farewell and a challenge to everyone present to make some sense of the mystery of life and death.

For all our sophistication and technological achievement, what do we truly know about death? Little more, perhaps, than our Stone Age and Bronze Age ancestors. It is always when we stand in the presence of death that we are at our most vulnerable and primitive. It is also the time when, like the Shetlanders of old, we look for hope in death. A fertility religion which sees death as the forerunner of birth offers hope. Christians, on the other hand, find hope in the promise of eternal life through the sacrifice of Jesus. The Christian view has not superseded the old; it has added to it and enhanced it. In practice

Christianity, while retaining its uniqueness, has synchronized with the rituals of former beliefs; from its early days, church practice was linked to the cycles of the year. The liturgical year mirrors the natural year:

Midwinter, which to many pre-Christians was seen as the time when the earth lay gripped by a deathly sleep, is Christmas time – the festival when Christians celebrate the birth of Jesus.

Spring coincides with Easter and is when the world comes to life again. Easter celebrates the resurrection of Jesus from the dead. Our modern-day images associated with Easter, indeed the name Easter itself, date from pre-Christian times: Easter bunnies are the successors of our ancestors' magic hares, and eggs were an ancient icon of birth. The new growth of spring, when the new leaves appear on the trees, was depicted by many medieval artists as the green man. He is shown as a face sprouting leaves and branches and the image is found in older church buildings and cathedrals around Britain and Europe.

All Hallows' Eve, the night before the feast of All Hallows when the dead are remembered in the Christian Calendar, has popularly become Hallowe'en. It is that dark time of autumn when, in Europe and North America, death has overshadowed the natural world. In myth it is the time when the veil separating the world of the living and that of the dead is lifted. It is when the spirits walk the earth again, and the rites of Hallowe'en are those of protection and propitiation.

The people of the modern developed world are rapidly losing touch with the rhythms and realities of nature which lie behind the festivals of the year. Night can be turned to day at the flick of an electric light switch. Winter can be turned to summer with central heating. Distances which took our ancestors months to travel can be crossed in hours. Christmas is celebrated in centrally heated shopping centres and Hallowe'en has been turned into a children's carnival.

It is interesting to note how Hallowe'en has grown in importance as our contact with the rhythms of nature has declined. A case could be made for saying that the growth of the former compensates or substitutes for the decline in the latter. It is as if, once a year, children are given special permission to explore the hidden world of fear. It is done in a supervised manner and children are often accompanied by a responsible adult when they call from house to house to 'trick or treat'. They dress themselves as ghosts, skeletons, spooks and witches and are given a licence to frighten themselves and each other. Many Christians fear that the practice not only borders on the Pagan, but also exposes young minds to the occult. The practice can be defended by saying that children need to explore the fears inside them. In the same way that children need to be allowed to discover their full physical capabilities under trained and responsible instruction, so they need to explore the boundaries of the mind and the imagination in a safe way. It could be said that celebrating Hallowe'en under the eye of a caring adults is as important to a child's spiritual education as learning how to swim is to a child's physical development – as long as the child is under the guidance of an experienced instructor.

In making huge technological strides we have gained much, but are we in danger of losing an innate understanding of the world – an intuitive wisdom which our ancestors appear to have had? They viewed death as part of the whole experience of being human. We view death as failure. It comes when medical expertise reaches its limits. Yet, however we regard death today, however much we are determined to erase the wisdoms of the past, we cannot avoid the simple fact that like all living humans and everyone who has gone before, each one of us will die. Death remains as the destination towards which we are all born to journey.

And while we may attempt to delay death as much as possible, we all must eventually meet it face to face. Death can be described as the final and unavoidable submission. It involves the acceptance that human ingenuity and technology ultimately have their limitations. At the time of death we are as naked and powerless as our ancestors. As they were in life, so we are today, profoundly ignorant of what lies ahead.

CHAPTER TWO

Death of the Body

There are some matters concerning death about which we in the modern world can rightly claim to have superior knowledge compared with that of our ancestors. These are the issues involving the sciences of death, the biology, physics and chemistry of that process whereby a living and loving person turns into a lifeless and unresponsive corpse.

Medical science reveals far more about the many causes of death than medical folklore ever did. We know how to treat the majority of the common diseases which once would have been fatal. Smallpox, tuberculosis, scarlet fever, pneumonia, measles – the killers of the past, the diseases our ancestors feared – are now almost entirely eradicated or eminently curable. We can delay death more effectively than any generation before us.

However, through our ability to delay death or, to put it another way, prolong life, new problems have arisen. The first was touched upon earlier: within the bounds of modern medicine, the failure to find a cure for a condition is viewed as overall failure. Yet finding the way to prolong life is only one part of dealing with death. Another aspect is planning a good death. While hope is maintained, whether false or genuine, that a cure is possible, little attention is given to planning the death. Sometimes the medical intervention required to maintain the appearance of hope is so unpleasant and invasive that quality of life is drastically impaired. Only when the inevitable is accepted is it possible to turn a failure into an opportunity – ideas to be explored later in the book.

The second problem arising from the advances of modern medicine lies in the assumption that progress is linear and constant. We assume that as life expectancy has risen in the twentieth century, it will carry on rising. Ultimately, it is implied, technology will have pushed death back so far that future generations will expect to be immortal. This is not only an unlikely event, but an undesirable possibility. We are already seeing that certain medical advances are unsustainable. Antibiotics, the wonder drugs of the twentieth century, are sidestepped by nature after a while. New variations on the antibiotics have to be constantly formulated to keep ahead of the new strains of mutating superbugs. Also there are huge economic pressures imposed by a new demographic order when the retired, and eventually dependent, elderly outnumber the younger generation. And anyway, do we truly want to live for ever, or at least for many additional decades? This is a world of joy and sorrow and some people have more than their fair share of sorrow. Would they want to stay around for century after century without hope of respite? To the Flying Dutchman of Wagner's opera, condemned to sail the seas for ever, immortality was a curse.

Nevertheless there is now an industry dedicated to the preservation of corpses in a deep-frozen state, which aims at thawing and reviving bodies sometime in the future. The idea is that when medical scientists have discovered a cure for the condition which caused the death of a particular person, their frozen body will be brought back to life and the cure applied. Cryonics is established in the United States where several corpses are already being held in suspended animation. There, a non-profit-making organization called Alcor pioneered the business. Ideally the scheme works in this way: when a client is dying, the suspension team races to the deathbed and rapidly transfers the corpse to a cooling stretcher. From there it is taken to a cryocapsule where it will remain until the day comes for reanimation. In a promotional leaflet Alcor described what the client would then experience in that event: 'Just a little over a year from the start of the revival procedure, the patient awakens in a hospital bed. A familiar voice calls out his name. Instantly there is recognition. It is his wife. But she is not as she was. She is young and beautiful again. More beautiful even than he remembered.' According to this, both the client and his wife will have been transformed by science, which by that time will have found the secret of eternal youth. What happens to those who opt for the cut-price deal, in which only the head is preserved, can be left to the grisly imagination.

The art, or science, of cryonics has not yet been perfected. It is doubtful if it ever will be. The idea that real-life Rip van Winkles can buy themselves a passage to the future is very dubious. There are many legal and ethical questions to be sorted out. What if it were shown that the best results were to be obtained by freezing just before natural death? Would that be murder? Would corpses survive hundreds of years? What if the freezers broke down? What if the thawing process resulted in brain damage? Would thoughts and memories survive the deep-freeze? These are all practical concerns which the cryo-enthusiasts dismiss. They say that the story of Jesus reviving Lazarus gives cryonics biblical justification. They say that one day every town will have its cryonics centre in the way that today every town has a crematorium and undertaker's business. They even say that the potential problem of over-population need not be a hurdle. There are plenty of ways of controlling the birth rate, they say, enough to allow everyone who wants to live for ever to do so without crowding the planet.

But fantasy aside, a real and more tangible problem that arises from the ability to defer death is that of definition. The boundary between life and death is becoming harder to draw. The moment of death is harder to pinpoint. We can no longer be certain that the old definitions of death hold true. Certainly a corpse from which life has long departed is unmistakeable. It is stiff and cold. If it has been lying undisturbed for a while it will have been disfigured by decomposition and be smelling very unpleasant. However, in the first hours after death, before reaching even the early stage of decay, the corpse will have gone through a process, rather than an event, called death.

The body is made up of cells, but they are not of identical types, and each type dies at a different rate when deprived of oxygenated blood. The knee-jerk reaction lasts for twenty minutes after death – a fact confirmed by tests carried out on French prisoners executed by guillotine. Muscles continue to react to electrical stimulation for several minutes. A kidney for transplantation can be kept chilled for several hours before being given to a recipient and, once attached to a new blood supply, can carry on living for years after the donor has died.

The practice of transplantation is one of the areas of medical advance which has given rise to problems of definition. A person who is identified as brainstem-dead by a standard series of response tests, and from whom transplanted organs may legally be taken, does not appear to be dead in the traditional sense. The corpse remains warm, as breathing and blood flow are artificially maintained. There is a visible heartbeat and the chest rises and falls. However, when the tests for brainstem-death are carried out, the medical team find no response – not even the automatic reflexes in the eye. The tests are designed to find any evidence that the brain is functioning, either consciously or unconsciously. Death was once defined as the permanent cessation of the vital organs; now it is possible and legal to describe a person as dead even though the vital organs remain in operation.

The ambiguity produces a new variation on a primitive fear. Might the doctors, in their eagerness to get organs, assume someone is dead before they have in fact crossed the threshold from life irrevocably? In former times one of the common horrors associated with death was also that a person's death might be misdiagnosed. As a consequence many people took elaborate precautions against the hazards of premature burial. Even then it was a remote possibility, but the fear existed as a phobia for some – both extreme in intensity and irrational in form. In the nineteenth century in some parts of Europe, facilities such as bell pulls were placed in vaults and graves so that anyone prematurely buried could raise the alarm.

Francis Douce, who died in 1834, left £200 in his will to a famous surgeon who would, 'sever my head or extract my heart from my body, so to prevent any possibility of the return of vitality'.[1] His father, also Francis Douce, had had the same fear and requested that on his death his body was to remain above ground for two weeks. It was only with the introduction of arterial embalming in the 1880s and 1890s that premature burial became a thing of the past. Once a corpse was embalmed there was no earthly chance it could rise from the dead.

Modern science has found other ways to complicate issues of definition further. We now know that literally, as The Book of Common Prayer says, 'in the midst of life we are in death'. From the moment of birth parts of us are dying. It is quite obvious that the man of fifty is not the same as the boy of ten he once was, forty years earlier. Apart from the teeth, almost every part of the body has been replaced several times over in that period. In an average lifetime a person sheds around three stone of dead skin. Hair drops out, blood cells cease to function, nails are cut, and all this material is replaced. One of the most persuasive arguments that personality exists in some way independent from, as well as dependent on, the body, is that of ageing. A toothless old man is still capable of having the same thoughts he did when a strapping youth, yet not a single cell in his ageing body has survived from that of fifty years before. The spirit may continue to be willing, but the flesh gets progressively weaker.

The writer George Bernard Shaw raised the teasing possibility that because, as he claimed, every cell in the body was replaced every seven years, no one should be held responsible for offences they had committed more than seven years earlier when they were, basically, an entirely different person. However, it is now accepted that Shaw was not correct in the details of his assumption. While almost all cells are indeed regularly replaced, certain essential ones, including heart-muscle cells and some nerve cells, are not. They simply die off gradually, which rather complicates Shaw's argument.

The definition of death is not the only issue thrown up by the modern scientific quest to prolong life. If death is seen as a failure of medicine, then relatives, doctors and the State want to know why failure occurred. Is someone to blame? Today, in the developed Western world, once death is finally recognized, much importance is attached to identifying the cause. In Britain, the legal document, the death certificate, which confirms that a person is officially 'deceased' must give a cause of death signed by a qualified medical practitioner. It is not satisfactory for the certificate to say that a person died of old age – the precise cause must be stated. It is as if to say that death is not a natural end of life, but an abnormality.

When an accident happens in most modern Western countries there has to be an inquiry. 'Misfortune' is not a satisfactory answer to give to the question, Why did death occur? Often there is a demand to know who was to blame. Following the 1999 earthquake in Turkey, when tens of thousands of people were killed, scapegoats were found from within the building and construction industry. They were accused of building poor-quality homes which collapsed when the earth moved from seismic pressure. When Princess Diana died in the Paris car crash of 1997, two years of painstaking inquiry were initiated to establish the precise sequence of events which led to the crash and to determine who was largely responsible for the outcome. In the course of this inquiry the French legal authorities decided that the blame, which had been popularly and instantly attached to the posse of chasing photographers, should be attached instead to the driver of the car who had allegedly been drinking alcohol. At its best this quest for cause can also be a quest for justice, but at its worst it can be bitterly destructive, especially when it hinders the grieving process or encourages prolonged and damaging litigation.

There is also the tendency today to see those who die as victims, rather than people who have gone through the last of this earthly life's experiences. Of course some who die are victims: those who are murdered are victims. But is it correct to talk of cancer victims or AIDS victims? As Frank Furedi observed,

> In today's world, it is evident that victimhood and suffering represent a moral claim on society. The grounds on which victimhood represents a moral claim is not what you did, but what has been done to you. In a society where human action is regarded with suspicion, suffering is one of the few experiences with which everyone can feel comfortable. Indeed, suffering has replaced conscious action as the experience of real meaning. More and more, suffering is depicted as having some purpose for which one is entitled to be rewarded or compensated.[2]

Frank Furedi went on to suggest that society actually encourages those who suffer to seek some meaning in their experience. The media, he suggests, portray personal tragedy as moral plays in which a special significance is attributed to the victim's loss. When tragedy strikes and family members are subjected to the macabre ritual of media interview, they invariably express the hope that their 'loved one had not died in vain... A tragic death is swiftly transformed into a cause. Swiftly a charity is set up to make sure that others learn the lessons of the tragedy.'[3] Society implies in this that death has no other intrinsic meaning. A tragedy is a warning, is the message, and death is purposeless.

If science attributes no purpose to death, it can still learn from the debris of death, although the knowledge acquired is technical and historical. It is possible, through the recent developments in the science of pathology, to tell a great deal about the past from the evidence offered by the remains of the dead. Both archaeology and criminal investigation have benefited enormously from the new skills and techniques which the pathologists have adopted. For instance, DNA fingerprinting has given the forensic pathologist a significant new tool when it come to identifying a mutilated or fire-damaged corpse. At one time samples of fibre, blood, soil or other material found with human remains had to be isolated in reasonable quantities in order to be analyzed. Today microscopic samples yield important clues.

Fictional pathologists have now become the stars of television 'who-dunnits'. No modern crime book or drama is complete without the pathologist emerging as a major character in the plot, especially if she is female and attractive. The post-mortem has become a source of entertainment again. Where once distinguished anatomists dissected the corpses of paupers or criminals in operating 'theatres' before tiered benches of students, today autopsies in white-tiled and stainless-steel mortuaries are the settings for television dramas. Archaeologists, not to be outdone, often appear on television with ancient skulls, and with the help of experienced sculptors recreate the faces of our ancestors.

There is huge interest in death, even the unpleasant aspects, as long as they are sanitized in their presentation and kept at arm's length from reality. Clean, fictional death is one thing; what most people in the West do not know about, and do not want to know about, are the true facts of death. Treating accident victims, handling dead bodies and disposing of the dead are left to the professionals. At one time the village carpenter was also the undertaker because he had the skills and materials to make coffins. There was always a local person, or family member, who knew about preparing a corpse for burial. Today there are several classes of people who are the death specialists. Undertaking is a full-time occupation with its own training programmes in funeral management and embalming. The industry, like any other, has its own career structures. Funeral directors are often members of large business corporations. For a fee they take over the disposal of the corpse and the arrangement of ritual. They offer their services as a product, looking for any added value in the form of a more elaborate coffin, or a more ostentatious funeral procession, to help their profits. This whole area of the death business will be explored in more detail in a later chapter.

Other death professionals include paramedics, police officers, firefighters who deal with the debris of accidents, coroners, registrars and bereavement counsellors. There are even specialist homes and hospitals where people go to die. As a result little is known by the ordinary person in the street about the way a body stops functioning at the end of life and what processes then occur after death. Modern dying, as identified by Dr Sherwin Nuland, shields almost all of us. Yet even modern dying cannot produce a uniform death. In the way that no face is identical in every respect to another, no two people share the exact same death. Dying is a singular and individual experience. The way we die and the age at which we die depend on several factors, most notably our genetic make-up, gender, social class and the place where we live.

It is also the case that more deaths by natural causes occur in the small hours of the morning than at at any other time of day. Everyone has a built-in twenty-four-hour biological cycle and during sleep, especially in the hours between midnight and dawn, the body's rate of metabolic activity is at its lowest. Women live, on average, longer than men. People in the developed world live longer than those in the developing world. People whose parents die young tend also to die young. In the Bible, the life of man is given as three-score years and ten – seventy. A British citizen born today can, on average, expect to live seventy-four years if male and eighty years if female. Within a generation over 10 per cent of the population of Britain will be aged seventy-five or over. A small few might even exceed the age of 110. Life expectancy in a country like Uganda, however, is little more than forty years.

The most common causes of death worldwide, including those which might simply be attributed to old age, are:

infectious and parasitic disease (representing 33 per cent of the total);
heart disease and strokes (29 per cent);
cancer (12 per cent);
death at the time of birth from one of several causes of infant death
    (7 per cent);

chronic lung disease (6 per cent);
accidents, murder or suicide (2 per cent);
malnutrition (2 per cent).[4]

Omitted from the figures above are those deaths of people who were victims of war or massacre. In the twentieth century some 110 million people died as a result of conflict between nations or tribes.

The category of infectious and parasitic disease represents a sad catalogue of avoidable misery. Four million children a year under the age of five die from lung infections which are easily treatable. Tuberculosis, almost unknown as a killer in Britain for many years, although now making a comeback, accounts for the deaths of 3 million people a year worldwide. Eight thousand children a day die from diarrhoeal infections. Put more simply, these millions of avoidable deaths are caused by poverty. Babies who die at or near to birth are most frequently, too, the victims of poverty. Three hundred thousand children a year die from tetanus, having been born in unhygienic surroundings without any of the benefits of modern sanitation or medical knowledge.

One day each of us will become a mortality statistic. We will be slotted into one of the categories of death and we all hope that the category will not be one of the most fearful. So what will that final moment be like? It depends on whether one goes out with a bang or a whimper. The event is one we might try to defer, but we cannot cancel it, despite the quip of the American comedian Woody Allen, 'It's not that I am afraid of dying. I just don't want to be there when it happens.'

There is one comforting thought: much evidence suggests that the body provides its own natural sedative at the time of traumatic death. It is suggested that it is something common to all sentient animals which might find themselves some other animal's prey. The famous missionary Dr Livingstone was once attacked by a lion in Africa and thought that his last moment had come. Later he described how he had felt in the face of danger:

Growling horribly close to my ear, he shook me as a terrier dog does a rat. The shock produced a stupor similar to that which seems to be felt by a mouse after the first shake of the cat. It caused a sort of dreaminess, in which there was no sense of pain nor feeling of terror, though quite conscious of all that was happening... The shake annihilated fear, and allowed no sense of horror in looking round at the beast. This peculiar state is probably in all animals killed by carnivora; and if so, is a merciful provision by our benevolent Creator for lessening the pain of death.[5]

A similar sensation of calm has been described by many trauma victims. Soldiers injured in war often report how they felt no pain from their injuries in the heat of battle. It is generally attributed to the effect of the body's self-generated opiates, the endorphins. The surgeon Bertram Owen Smith was himself badly injured during the Second World War. He became a member of the exclusive Guinea Pig Club, the club of airmen who were treated by the plastic surgeon Archibald McIndoe. Owen Smith was piloting a Whitley bomber, known in the RAF as the Flying Coffin, which crash-landed. He realized when the plane came to a halt that he was still alive, but there was a fire and he was being burned. He and his two fellow aircrew members, the second pilot and the wireless operator, kicked at the window. They hammered at it and eventually got it open and squeezed out. Owen Smith recalls being aware of the fact that he was on fire, but didn't feel any pain. 'Thank God I was still wearing my flying gloves,' he said later when reviewing his wounds. Despite severe burns to his face, his hands were not damaged and he went on to become a surgeon, treating war victims in central Africa.

I only knew we'd been in that aircraft longer than we'd wanted to be. And I also knew that there was an awful lot of explosion still to come. So we just ran. And, fortunately, we ran in the right direction. Past the tail of the aircraft and straight into the river.

Which not only put out the flames but, because we were now standing on the river bed behind the river bank, protected us when the Whitley went up. And how it went up.

You know, it's amazing what the body will stand. I know it was dark but I can honestly say that I didn't realize I was badly burned. When the bangs and pops finished, we staggered out of the shallow river and made our way across the field and people came to meet us as they heard us chattering and stumbling away. And only then did I begin to feel a bit of pain. So I said, and I remember this, 'Please could you take us to the nearest doctor,' very politely. And they did. And a very unhappy village medico, who obviously saw how seriously we were burned, had to cope with us.[6]

Even when the body is faced with its sudden demise from internal, rather than external factors, the mind need not panic. One man, who dropped from a massive heart attack while playing tennis and who would have died but for immediate medical intervention, has described the experience vividly. He recalled no pain, just the slow collapse of his body: 'And then the lights went out... as if you flip a switch. The only difference from that was that it was in slow motion. The change from light to dark was very evident, but the speed with which it happened was gradual. I was aware that I'd collapsed. I felt like somebody took the life out of me. I felt shrunk... like a deflated balloon.'[7]

Does the body similarly calm itself when death approaches after a long illness? The witness at the deathbed might suppose not, for death is often preceded by a struggle. Just before the point of clinical death is reached, the dying person appears to be battling for life. It can be distressing to watch. Many doctors, however, believe that the patient remains unconscious of what is going on. By that time the oxygen deficiency in the brain will have rendered the patient unaware of surroundings and events. The physician Dr Sherwin Nuland has written that the dying person is too far gone to be aware of the apparent death agonies which the onlookers witness. He believes that much of what occurs is not a response to pain or mental anguish, but due simply to muscle spasms induced by the blood's terminal acidity:

> The apparent struggles of the agonal moments are like some violent outburst of protest arising deep in the primitive unconscious, raging against the too-hasty departure of the spirit… The ultimate agonal moment… is accompanied either by the cessation of breathing or by a short series of great heaving gasps; on rare occasions there may be other movements as well, such as the violent tightening of [the] laryngeal muscles into a terrifying bark. Simultaneously, the chest or shoulders will sometimes heave once or twice and there may be a brief agonal convulsion. The agonal phase merges into clinical death, and thence into the permanence of mortality.[8]

Another description of the process of dying comes from Professor Cedric Mims:

> Departure from life can be silent and peaceful, or so it seems, to the observer, but sometimes the final moments are more turbulent… muscles go into spasms and it may look as if a real death struggle is in process. The face twitches, breathing becomes difficult and a 'death rattle' is occasionally heard. There may be a brief convulsion before, with a series of heavy gasps and a final expiration, the body relaxes and is still. The person 'has expired'. Hearing is the last sense to go, so it is kind to hold a dying person's hand and talk to him.[9]

When the process of dying is extended, as it was with my father who died several weeks after the stroke which precipitated his death, watching it is not easy. The dying person stays asleep for long periods of time, but when the eyes open and the person is aware of what is going on around him or her, the words can be quite lucid. Talking to his

40

granddaughter, my father remembered a game he used to play when she was a child – saying the alphabet backwards. Unaided he started at Z and recited the letters back to A. At other times he called out for a nurse with the urgency one normally hears only from a child. What was going on in his mind as he slept, one can only speculate. Was he dreaming of the past or was he starting out on his way to something beyond? Kathleen Dowling Singh writes of the nearing-death experience as the intake of food declines and the sleep patterns return to those of an infant:

> Those who have been able to share verbally, and sometimes non-verbally, with me throughout this stage of the process have indicated something of the profound changes they are undergoing in their own deep interior. While to outside observation they appear to be 'depressed', withdrawn, or merely sleeping, this is, in fact, the quality of 'positive depression' of the Nearing-Death Experience, a deep turning inward to access beyond.[10]

She describes the outward symptoms of what she calls 'terminal agitation' and 'restlessness' and says that dying patients can find comfort in therapeutic touch or from music such as the antiphonal music of the Christian monastic tradition, used as a preparation for death.

One explanation as to how music can be of value is presented by the music teacher Judith Marten-Meynell, who uses voice and harp to create music for the dying: 'The tones and vibrations of the harp are assimilated through the skin of the body and help to unbind the patient, assisting them in letting go of earthly ties, preparing them for their journey to a different level of consciousness.'[11]

If, much closer to death, the patient wakes in a state of seeming disorientation, he or she may appear to be confused as to time, place and identity. Kathleen Dowling Singh suggests, from her observations, that the person who is about to die goes through a process whereby they relearn and restructure their understanding of time, place and identity. In the final moments of life the person may have already transcended, as she puts it, 'the level of consciousness of the mental ego'[12] in which, in all likelihood, his or her caregivers are operating. Early memories sometimes appear to flood into awareness at this point. This happens at the same time as the person withdraws from life. In other words, Singh is suggesting, as the carers watch and help the dying person through their final hours or minutes of life, the dying person may have already set out on the journey to the next world. He or she will have left behind the personality and thought processes they once needed in order to survive in the material world, and begun to adopt those more appropriate to the spiritual world. As this transition occurs the dying person experiences vivid recollections of their life – especially those associated with childhood, when they were learning how to cope in this world and forging their personality. This observation is endorsed by the beliefs of several other faiths. Tibetan Buddhists say that dying people go through a stage when they see themselves as they had been in life. 'My life flashed before my eyes,' some people have said who have been on the verge of dying, but later recovered.

One of the saddest and most mysterious of the death processes is that of Alzheimer's disease. I have known several people whose final years have been spent in that slow terminal decline and withdrawal when the personality appears to leech away from the body. Kathleen Dowling Singh's description above of the reintegration of the ego might apply to an Alzheimer's patient, but in slow motion. All the outward signs displayed by the patient in the early stages are of confusion and disorientation. A patient might be prone to irrationality, anger – even violence. Later the person enters a vegetative state. It is almost as if they are already dead, but that the body refuses to cooperate. Among the few things that make caring for an Alzheimer's patient bearable are the occasional glimpses of memory of past events shared. That this occurs is a sign that the mind has not entirely left the body. One can only suppose that the patient is existing in a strange limbo between this life and the next. In the final months there will be moments of calm, but before reaching that stage the Alzheimer's patient will have gone through several distressing stages. One of these stages will involve fantasy fears, for example that much trusted friends are stealing money. There is also the especially difficult stage when the patient is sufficiently aware of reality to know that they have the disease, but can do nothing about it.

Post-mortem examination of the brains of Alzheimer's patients reveals that the disease is associated with a physical deterioration of the brain itself. The disease, which is not just associated with old age, but can strike from middle-age onwards, occurs when the brain atrophies and the ventricles expand. This identifiable physical cause raises interesting questions concerning the personality: Does personality only exist as a function of brain activity? When the brain becomes damaged by trauma or disease, is the personality then also damaged? Does one's conscious being, in all its sensitive and complex depth, exist entirely in the brain? When the brain stops, does our very being cease to exist? From outward symptoms this would appear to be the case. The personality of the patient with Alzheimer's disease appears, when judged by all outward criteria, to be affected to a degree which directly correlates to the extent of the observable brain damage.

Yet there is counter-evidence to suggest that even after brain damage, when a patient is demonstrating alarming signs of disintegration, the hidden personality remains intact. People who suffer brain damage as a result of strokes may find their ability to speak severely curtailed. They will sometimes be under the impression that they are talking normally and expressing themselves lucidly, but the damaged brain contorts their words. They will want to use a word, say, 'cup', and believe that they have used it correctly in a sentence, yet the word will be heard by the listener as, say, 'tree'. Dr Sherwin Nuland tells the story of the man with brain damage who says to his wife, 'The train is late, please could you do something about it?' She replies, 'But we're not waiting for a train.' He points to his feet with irritation: 'Look, can't you see? The train's late.' It then occurs to her that what he means is that his shoelaces are undone. He has unknowingly used the wrong words and becomes cross when she fails to understand what to him is a straightforward request.[13]

If the brain is seen as the vehicle whereby the personality interacts with, and makes sense of, the world, then it could be argued that when the brain is damaged it will leave the personality out of touch with the world, but otherwise unharmed. It would be like the driver of a car discovering that the brakes and steering had failed. The driver will be as competent at driving as ever, but the car will be unresponsive to his or her wishes, and appear to be out of control.

I remember once meeting a musician who had suffered brain damage that had removed his short-term memory. His life went round and round in the same loop and he was quite unaware of it. If his wife left his sight for one moment he would become anxious. When she returned he would ask her where she had gone and tell her how worried he had been. Then a few moments later he would lose sight of her again. He would become increasingly anxious and when she reappeared he would quiz her in exactly the same way yet again. The scene was re-enacted dozens of times every day. However, he could still play the piano, and on one occasion conducted a choir with all his old ability and personality, yet a few moments afterwards he had forgotten the whole episode.

Memory, both short-term and long-term, is essential if one is to have an appreciation of time. If that part of the brain which provides memory fails to function, then time is perceived to have ceased. Everything that happens does so in the perpetual now. If after death there is no time – at least no time as we know it and have to use it here on earth – then to live on earth without a sense of time must be a form of death. But it is a death which coexists with life and, as the example of the musician demonstrates, personality can survive the loss of the appreciation of time.

Music is one of the paths to transcendence, as are meditation, other art forms, prayer and worship. Transcendence occurs irrespective of and apart from time and space. It can be said that after death the soul transcends time and space. Transcendence, says Kathleen Dowling Singh, leads us in increasing splendour and in overwhelming glory to full and complete integration of the self with the spirit. 'At integration the power of the Ground of Being moves freely through the mindbody.'[14] Her choice of words to describe transcendence may not be those which would be chosen by someone from a Christian tradition, but she is essentially talking of the soul and of God. She does, however, borrow words from one familiar Christian blessing when she writes, 'The self is at deep and great peace in its integration with the Ground of Being. This is the peace which, literally, passeth all understanding.'[15]

The classic images of death do not focus on the possibility of transcendence. They consist mostly of images of material decay. The relic of the body's decay which survives the longest is the skeleton. The skull in particular, the home of the mind and the foundation on which the face was built, is a very potent symbol of death. In some parts of Brittany, once the dead have been in their graves long enough for the flesh to have disintegrated, the bones are exhumed and placed together with the bones of friends and foes alike, in an ossuary. It is as if, at one and the same time, the Bretons wish to appear to be on familiar terms with their ancestors and to exhibit no fear of death, and yet keep the bones on show as a reminder of their own mortality and the futility of pursuing the pleasures of the flesh.

One reason why the hospice movement has developed in recent years in the Western world, and especially in Britain, is that modern hospitals dispensing scientific medicine ignore the spiritual aspect of dying. It is part of the process of modern dying that death is seen as the enemy to be kept at bay. Consequently the dying person, progressing naturally through the nearing-death experience, is often subjected to the increasingly hopeless, invasive medical procedures mentioned earlier. In the hospice setting modern palliative treatments are offered, but in conjunction with that care, hospice workers are offering more. Many of them are people motivated by faith. They find that as they strengthen and comfort the dying with their own expressions of hope, they in turn have their faith supported by the people for whom they are caring.

One remarkable illustration of this comes from St Joseph's Hospice at Thornton on Merseyside. In 1981 a 44-year-old man, Les, was admitted who impressed everyone at the Roman Catholic-run hospice with his remarkable holiness. The director, Father Francis O'Leary, described Les as charismatic. His holiness was not expressed in anything specific that he did nor in any pious words he said, but in his general demeanour. When Les died the nurses found his image imprinted on the mattress of his bed. 'It was like the Turin Shroud,' says Father O'Leary.[16] Something physical can happen at the point of death, he believes, which is like a transfiguration. It is miraculous and associated only with people of exceptional holiness, he says. It is so intense that it can leave an image behind.

It is open to debate whether such a transfiguration can happen. What can be said with more certainty is that the ethos of the typical modern hospital is not conducive to nurturing the spiritual side of death. It can be argued that every death involves transcendence, even when those involved are not especially saintly. Yet it is rare in a busy modern scientific hospital for staff to have the time, training or interest in exploring the possibilities of transcendence with their dying patients. At best a hard-pressed chaplain will find time to say a prayer, a word of comfort, or offer the sacraments. In modern dying the spiritual aspects of death appear to be mostly ignored as the physical needs are seen to.

This is an area of concern for many involved with the dying and has of late become a matter for public debate. It is not the doctors who are the villains, although some today remain extraordinarily insensitive. Often the demand for more medical intervention at the end, to stave off the inevitable, comes from relatives and not the medical profession. Guidelines issued by the British Medical Association (BMA), in June

1999, suggested that doctors should be able to overrule a family's wish to keep a patient alive if they believe no further treatment could be of benefit. A co-author of the guidelines, Raanan Gillon, Professor of Medical Ethics at Imperial College, London, said that they could conflict with those who thought that just keeping someone alive was the goal of medicine. 'Just staying alive is no good unless it is a means to an end. If not, then it is normally reasonable to withdraw... the intent is not to kill but to allow someone to die with compassion.'[17]

The guidelines were criticized as euthanasia by the back door. But the courts had already set the tone of the debate in Britain, where the House of Lords, in 1993, had ruled that medical staff caring for a young man, Tony Bland, who had been in a persistent vegetative state since the Hillsborough football-ground disaster of 1987, would be allowed to withdraw artificial feeding and hydration. Many doctors have argued strongly for the minimum amount of legislation in the area. To legalize euthanasia, they say, could herald extensive abuse. Far better to leave the law alone and let doctors act with discretion and in confidence when they offer to assist a patient at the point of death.

One fear is that deaths of those in the final stages might be planned for the efficiency of the staff. Births in many maternity units are now induced to fit the convenience of staff rotas. Why not deaths? 'Mr Jones is bound to die this week; let's make it Thursday as that will be most convenient for the hospital mortuary.'

If death is a natural process through which a person travels to reach a transcendent state, then important events could well be going on within that person's mind as they lie unconscious in a hospital bed. To cut short that process with death-inducing drugs for administrative convenience might be far more harmful than would appear on the surface. The BMA guidelines suggest that the first factor to be borne in mind in determining whether extended treatment would benefit a patient is the patient's own view. The patient's own wishes and values are to be ascertained. The likelihood of the treatment causing pain has to be taken into account and the level of awareness the individual has of his or her existence or surroundings must also be determined. This last factor is the difficult one when it comes to the final stages of dying. A wise doctor would probably only step in to relieve pain if the patient had seemed to be unaware of their surroundings for some considerable period, and the question of withholding treatment or nutrition would only apply in this case.

In practice, too, a wise jury acquits doctors who appear to have ended a patient's life by their actions, but with the best of intentions, and can differentiate between them and cold-blooded murderers such as Dr Harold Shipman. GP Dr David Moor was acquitted by Newcastle Crown Court in May 1999 on a charge of murdering an 85-year-old patient. He had increased the level of diamorphine administered to his patient to relieve his pain. It took a jury of eight women and four men little more than an hour to unanimously find the doctor not guilty.

I shall now return from discussing the ethical questions associated with dying to describing the physical event. In many cases, even if the heart has stopped beating, it does not mean that that person is beyond resuscitation. When a person has had a sudden heart failure or, for example, has been pulled from the water having stopped breathing, it is possible, using resuscitation techniques, to restart breathing and a heartbeat. This can be done by electrical stimulation – defibrillation – as well as manual massage and 'the kiss of life' – mouth-to-mouth breathing.

If all this fails, then the body completes its process of shutting down, and decomposition will start. For the first three hours or so the corpse remains warm and limp. Then muscles begin to contract and the corpse stiffens. This is rigor mortis. The stiffness remains for another thirty-six hours approximately. By the end of this time, the body becomes limp again. Depending upon the surroundings, the body will have cooled down to match the ambient temperature by about eight hours after death. At the time of death, body fluids and stomach contents can leak and the underside of the body can become discoloured. Blood settles there due to gravity once the circulation ceases. The eyes take on a distinctive appearance as the corneas become cloudy and the eyeballs sink into their sockets. The contraction of the tiny muscles that cause hair to stand on end, plus the shrinking of the skin, gives a false impression that hair continues to grow after death.

The microbiologist Professor Cedric Mims has described the next invisible stage when some of the countless microbes in the intestines which are still alive spread through the body. The first parts to putrefy as the microbes invade the inner regions of the body are the intestines: 'The body breaks down as enzymes and other chemicals are released from dead tissues. The pancreas digests itself... Green substances and gas are produced in the tissues and the skin takes on a green or bluish colour and develops blisters.' Professor Mims gives a gruesome description of what happens next: 'The blisters may expand into large sacs of fluid... the front of the body swells up, the tongue can protrude from between the teeth... the corpse becomes an unpleasant sight... In temperate countries this stage is reached after four to six days and a disagreeable odour of hydrogen sulphide and methane is released.'[18]

The early stages of decomposition can be put on hold by embalming. This practice is carried out if a body is to be shown to the family over a period of time, or if the funeral is delayed. Embalmers like to think of creating from the corpse a beautiful memory of the living person for mourners to cherish. Embalming normally involves draining blood from the body and substituting an embalming fluid. It is an ancient practice which modern science has refined. After embalming, the corpse may be dressed in special clothes associated with the dead person, the hair brushed and set, and make-up applied. The most famous example of the embalmers' art is to be found in the mausoleum in Moscow where Lenin is on show. The Russian embalmers, who have to restore and update their charge from time to time, are viewed as the world-experts in long-term body preservation.

Longer-term storage of corpses is carried out in temperature-controlled cabinets. On the same principle as applies to refrigerated food, decay is delayed more and more as the temperature falls. This means is so effective that dead Arctic explorers, when discovered after many years entombed in the polar ice, look little different from the day when the cold, hunger and scurvy claimed them. In very rare cases it is claimed that the earthly remains of certain individuals of great sanctity do not decay normally. The bodies of St Bernadette of Lourdes and St Catherine of Genoa are, for instance, said to be incorruptible and they have survived intact.

Normally, without the retarding effects of embalming or extraordinary sanctity, the rate of decomposition will depend upon whether or not the corpse is buried, and at what depth. If the corpse is left exposed to the air, after a murder perhaps, ants, maggots and carrion-eaters will have their fill. 'The worms go in and the worms come out. They go in thin and they come out stout,' reveals one nasty playgound ditty, the worms, in this case, being maggots. Without the help of the army of scavengers and body-eaters, tissues liquify. In wet conditions body fats may become greasy and waxy, turning greenish-white in colour and smelling of cheese. And so the gruesome description goes on. Only cremation or embalming can thwart the inevitable course of nature. Decay is as natural to this created world as birth and without the minerals and organic compounds released by decay into the soil and food chain, nothing could be newly made.

Nothing stays still in nature. The weather keeps moving, water is constantly recycled and every atom of every element has been used and reused over and over again throughout the history of the world. To contemplate the notion in wonder, one only has to think that in all statistical probability, every one of us has eaten food containing atoms eaten as food by many of the great names in history – including Jesus himself. We have reused, in our own breathing, the same oxygen atoms that were inhaled by Christ and his apostles.

Bodily decay, however, is a topic which still belongs to the silent margins of discussions on death, unless the subject is used for dramatic purpose in a fictional detective story. 'Though death is far from being a taboo subject,' wrote Professor Douglas Davies, 'certainly in terms of media presentation and discussion, decay remains the unspoken word. Even so, it is not absent from private imagination.'[19]

In their survey on attitudes to death, to be explored more fully later, Professor Davies and his co-author Alastair Shaw found that ninety-six men (13 per cent of the survey) and 152 women (18 per cent) thought that others might prefer cremation because they would dislike the idea of the body rotting or of worms devouring it. When a direct question was put to respondents, however, 81 per cent said that they had no fear of decomposition. Barely 1 per cent of the entire sample admitted having been put off the idea by the images of rotting corpses in horror films or ghost stories. While people clearly differentiate between fact and fiction, there is nevertheless a minority who feel uncomfortable when contemplating the final decomposition of themselves or others.

Benjamin Franklin took the whole idea of his decomposition in a light-hearted spirit when he wrote his own epitaph:

> The body of
> Benjamin Franklin, printer
> (like the cover of an old book,
> Its contents worn out,
> And stript of its lettering and gilding),
> Lies here, food for worms!
> Yet the work itself shall not be lost,
> For it will, as he believed, appear once more,
> In a new
> And more beautiful edition,
> Corrected and amended
> By its author![20]

CHAPTER THREE

Forbidden Knowledge?

The Elizabethan Francis Bacon once declared the true end of knowledge to be 'the discovery of all operations and possibilities of operations from immortality... to the meanest mechanical practice'.[1] And in a letter to his contemporary Lord Burleigh he wrote, 'I have taken all knowledge to be my province.'[2]

Renaissance man set in motion a train of thought that, in the Age of Reason, developed into a presumptuousness from which emerged one of the more absurd fallacies of recent times – that it is possible for all knowledge that exists to be acquired and understood by humankind. Even today this idea is still kept alive by some scientists. They cling onto the idea in hope, almost as a matter of faith, in the face of the evidence. For, in the twentieth century, hand in hand with the promises of science came the many disappointments. Nevertheless, there are still members of the scientific community who sincerely believe that, given the right approach, the right funds and the right equipment, one day all the secrets of the universe will be in the possession of the human mind.

There are several examples of this way of thinking that can be cited. There are still scientists pursuing the holy grail of cheap, unlimited fuel. There are others who are engaged in mapping the entire human gene profile who believe that this could be the key to the elimination of all inherited disease. They are typical of those members of the scientific community who believe passionately in the unstoppable progress of science and ignore doubters. In their dedication and enthusiasm they appear to overlook the problem that for almost every advance made by science there is a corresponding reversal. When the atom was split the dawn of the nuclear bomb arrived. When pesticides were developed that raised the yields of crops, many of them entered the food chain and turned out to be poisonous to humans and wildlife. When CFCs were launched, which enabled many people to have cheap access to refrigeration, unbeknown to the scientists they had released chemicals into the atmosphere which would ultimately cause a depletion of the ozone layer and allow an increased measure of harmful radiation to reach the earth's surface. The most recent example of how scientific discoveries can have their downside concerns the use of genetically modified plants for food, whose production may cause loss of bio-diversity.

The scientific optimists are driven by the vision that, one day, an overarching theory or formula will be discovered which will reveal and explain all there is to know about their subject. The idea, especially when stretched as far as to promise answers on a cosmic scale, is fallacious, and in fairness to Bacon he, too, realized its shortcomings, because one question defies all attempts to find an answer. It is a simple but awesome question. What happens after death? It is a question that defies the scientific methodology, which requires data to be measured and experiments to be repeatable. It may be that the question is not just a foolish one to attempt to ask, but also is in itself logically invalid. It may be like asking, How much does Wednesday weigh? Or, What smell does yellow have? Such questions are absurd. The question, What happens after death? might be an equally invalid question to pose. The reason for this lies in the possibility that at the point of death, time may cease to have any meaning or context.

We talk of eternity being infinite time. Perhaps it is not that at all, but rather comprises the absence of time. And if there is no time after death, then the question, What happens after death? becomes an absurd one to contemplate, for the word 'after' can only exist in relation to time. Was it these mysteries that the psalmist was striving to express in the familiar words, 'For a thousand years in thy sight are but as yesterday.'[3] These thoughts were echoed in the familiar hymn, 'O God, Our Help in Ages Past', composed by Isaac Watts many years later:

> A thousand ages in thy sight
>   Are like an evening gone,
> Short as the watch that ends the night
>   Before the rising sun.

The hymn ends with the line: 'Be thou our guard while troubles last, and our eternal home.'[4]

It was T.S. Eliot who wrote of the beginning often being the end, and that making an end is to make a beginning.[5] We all know that time plays tricks. When we are enjoying ourselves, time seems to fly by. When we are bored, time drags.

Variations in time have practical implications. Time, as we measure it here on earth, is based on Greenwich Mean Time but varies according to longitude. Try telephoning a friend in New York at 9 a.m. London time; he or she will be none too pleased at being woken up at four o'clock in the morning. In the early days of the railways, even the minor variations in time across Britain proved inconvenient. Cornish time is around a quarter of an hour later than London time, if judged by the position of the sun at noon. Operating a timetable to allow for every county's own time was too complicated and time in Britain came to be standardized. This happened as recently as the last century and when 'railway time' was introduced, as it was called at first, there were many locals who protested that it was an unnatural replacement of traditional custom and practice. Today the Greenwich time signal acts as central reference point for time. Its unfailing accuracy is assumed and very few people notice when its regularity is occasionally altered by scientists to allow for the fact that the earth's rotation is almost imperceptibly slowing down.

Thanks to Albert Einstein we also know that time is relative, though few people understand exactly what this means unless they are fluent in the language of mathematics. Speed is expressed as a relationship between distance and time – for example, miles per hour (mph) or feet per second. Physicists have demonstrated that nothing can exceed the speed of light; it is the absolute upper limit of speed. Yet it is also known that when two objects are heading towards each other on a direct collision course, their relative speeds are the sum of their individual speeds. Therefore, a train travelling at 50 mph towards another train travelling at the same speed in the opposite direction will have a speed of 100 mph in relation to the other.

Yet what happens when two objects each travelling at more than half the speed of light are heading towards each other? As the relative speeds of the two objects cannot be greater than the speed of light, then something has to give: time and space become warped. Thus the speed of one object relative to the other will be slower than might have been expected in order to be less than that of light. Einstein's great contribution to physics was his discovery that space and time should not be considered in separation, but considered to be one unified whole – spacetime. Furthermore, spacetime is not fixed, but can be contorted, expanded or contracted.

We might prefer to think of time being a constant, like the ticking of a perpetual, undeviating clock. Yet our subjective experience and the objective reasoning of science both suggest otherwise. It is not fanciful to speculate that something strange happens to time in the context of eternity, but exactly what happens is something we do not know. It may be that we do not have the intellectual ability ever to understand what happens.

We need time to govern life on earth and, understood in that way, we know that things happen in their own good time. There are appropriate times for events. 'There is a time for everything, and a season for every activity under heaven,' we are told by the writer of the book of Ecclesiastes.[6] Note the word 'under'. The writer did not choose the word 'in' when referring to heaven. The writer was examining the nature and implications of existence without a belief in an afterlife which would be spent in heaven. There is:

a time to be born and a time to die;
a time to plant and a time to uproot;
a time to kill and a time to heal;
a time to pull down and a time to build up;
a time to weep and a time to laugh;
a time for mourning and a time for dancing;
a time to scatter stones and a time to gather them;
a time to embrace and a time to refrain from embracing;
a time to seek and a time to lose;
a time to keep and a time to throw away;
a time to tear and a time to mend;
a time for silence and a time for speech;
a time to love and a time to hate;
a time for war and a time for peace.[7]

These grand and resounding lines of poetry overshadow the verses which follow. But they are equally important and the sections of scripture are interdependent. God, says the author of Ecclesiastes,

has given men a sense of time past and future, but no comprehension of God's work from beginning to end... For man is a creature of chance and the beasts are creatures of chance, and one mischance awaits them all: death comes to both alike. They all draw the same breath. Men have no advantage over beast... all came from the dust, and to the dust all return. Who knows whether the spirit of man goes upward or whether the spirit of the beast goes downward to the earth?[8]

Perhaps we have to accept that the nature, or form, of post-mortem chronology is unfathomable, even forbidden, knowledge. In the story of Adam and Eve in the Garden of Eden, there is a tree of the knowledge of good and evil to provide the answers as they relate to this life. Humankind has been provided with no comparable tree of knowledge, with fruit to eat to supply us with insights into the life to come. As much as we feel tempted to ask questions, there is no fruit we can pick and eat to reveal the answers. Which is perhaps just as well, for if there were such a fruit, and we acquired the knowledge, we would become only too aware of our current state of simplicity. We would realize our utter intellectual nakedness and inadequacy. Literally, the word 'occult' means 'hidden' or 'concealed' and when the word is used in relation to knowledge it acquires sinister overtones, with the suggestion that the search for hidden knowledge is sinful and can only be pursued without the protection of God.

The Venerable Bede, the historian and man of prayer from whose pen we know much about the history of Britain in the so-called Dark Ages of the first millennium, had a quest for facts. But he was content to concede the boundaries of knowledge:

> The present life of man on earth is like the flight of a single sparrow through the hall where, in winter, you sit with your captains and ministers. Entering at one door and leaving by another, while it is inside it is untouched by the wintry storm; but this brief interval of calm is over in a moment, and it returns to the winter whence it came, vanishing from your sight. Man's life is similar; and of what follows it, or what went before, we are entirely ignorant.[9]

The Apostle Paul warned of the arrogance of thinking that one could understand the mystery. Several of the philosophers of the Roman and

Hellenic world of his time claimed that they could, through reason, deduce what the world to come was like. The Stoics, who took their teaching from Zora of Citium, believed that through the application of logic, physics and ethics it was possible to arrive at a knowledge of the world and human purpose. Paul wrote in his letter to the Colossians, 'do not let your minds be captured by hollow and delusive speculations, based on traditions of man-made teaching and centred on the elemental spirits of the universe and not on Christ'.[10] Paul did not encourage the early Christians to spend too much time on speculation. Yet, despite his advice, subsequent generations have seldom held back from seeking the knowledge. That knowledge has remained elusive and each generation in turn has failed to comprehend that the question about life after death is beyond our intellectual capabilities.

This question is not, of course, constantly in our minds. We try to push it aside and have an ambiguous relationship with it. Yet, while we are often afraid to ask the question, we cannot always avoid doing so. It crops up without invitation at times of illness or bereavement. It is the uninvited guest at every wake.

Perhaps we should take the insights of the mystic John of the Cross to heart. What happens to us after death will not be altered by what we know about the afterlife in this world. Love does not depend on knowledge, and certainly the supreme love, that of God, is not withheld from those who are ill-educated or non-intellectual or who have not sought to investigate the little that is known about the afterlife.

God loves unconditionally, so Christians believe. He also knows all. Yet can humans be expected to love God if they do not know anything about God and what life in God's presence might be like after death? This question was posed by Father R.H.J. Steuart in his book, *The Mystical Doctrine of St John of the Cross*.[11]

Father Steuart claimed that it was commonly held that the human will was unable to love that of which the human understanding had no knowledge. In other words, it is impossible for someone to love something unless that person first knows what that something might be. 'But in a supernatural way,' Father Steuart argued, 'God can certainly infuse love and increase it without infusing and increasing distinct knowledge... Yea, many spiritual persons have experience of this; their love of God burns more and more, while their knowledge does not grow. Men may know little and love much... The will may drink of love while the understanding drinks in no fresh knowledge.'[12]

The modern equivalent of religious mysticism could be said to be quantum physics. In the way that the mystics needed both single-mindedness and training to reach a point of comprehension, so quantum physicists need persistence and intellect. Both, within their own disciplines, transcend, or at least overreach, the confines of the everyday world experienced by most people. The religious mystics come to identify the mysteries they discover with God. In doing so they discover new and deeper ways of comprehending God. The physicists, on the other hand, do not generally make the same identification. They identify what they reveal through their mathematics as being incompatible with the notion of God. They are right in one sense. The amazing complexities they describe through the language of mathematics bear no relationship to the God of traditional religion or iconography. Yet they would be wrong to suppose that the representation of God by religion and art is the only valid one. God may be described in many different languages and through a range of academic disciplines and cultures. I once attended a eucharist conducted entirely in Chinese. I did not understand a word and yet would not have presumed to suggest that the Chinese congregation had no understanding of God because they were not worshipping in English!

As Professor Stephen Hawking wrote in his bestseller, *A Brief History of Time*, 'So long as the universe had a beginning, we could suppose it had a creator. But if the universe is really completely self-contained, having no boundary or edge, it would have neither beginning nor end: it would simply be. What place, then, for a creator?'[13] He poses a question which seems valid until one starts asking more deeply what we mean by the word 'creator'. It is limited in meaning in our vocabulary, but need not be so limited in God's realm. John the

Evangelist pre-empted the question almost 2,000 years earlier: 'In the beginning was the Word, and the Word was with God, and the Word was God. The same was in the beginning with God. All things were made by him; and without him was not any thing made that was made.'[14]

If we stick rigidly to our limited concept of time we miss the endless possibilities of the universe, which was, so all the main monotheistic faiths believe, created by God in a way beyond our restricted understanding of time and space. Similarly if we stick rigidly to our earthly dependence on time, we cannot see beyond it. And yet we must live by time here on earth and our intellects do not have the capacity to picture what lies beyond. Even the physicists' mathematics only provides an allegorical representation of ideas that are beyond us.

It is not surprising that that which is beyond us, that which we cannot visualize, conceptualize, hold or control, is something of which we are fearful. We stand in awe of the magnitude of it all. We dare not allow our minds to reach out. It is all too unfamiliar and insecure.

In our attempts to hide from the questions about death, we skirt around the subject. In the English language there are far more euphemisms to describe human death than even the Monty Python team could dream up for their famous dead-parrot sketch. This sketch involved a customer returning to a pet shop to complain that he had been sold a dead bird. The Norwegian Blue, so the shopkeeper was emphatically told, was no more: 'It has ceased to be! It's expired and gone to meet its maker! This is a late parrot! It's a stiff! Bereft of life it rests in peace... pushing up the daisies! It's rung down the curtain and joined the choir invisible!'

For people, the words used are more gently and tenderly employed, though every bit as final. Gravestones up and down the country attest to loved ones who have 'fallen asleep', 'gone to their rest', or 'passed on'. Except in the context of providing dates and facts, few of those whose lives are briefly recorded on headstones are simply said to have died – and yet die is what they all did and death is what will come to all of us sooner or later. When even the public acknowledgment of death is hedged about in such protective language, and the realities of dealing with death are now left to the professionals, it is not surprising that most people in Western societies go for many months or years deferring the ultimate question, What does happen after death?

We know what happens in a physical sense; the process of decomposition is well known. Forensic pathologists can use their knowledge of post-mortem decay to deduce time and cause of death. We also know what happens after death to friends and relations left behind. They grieve and perform rituals to help them grieve. We also see more violent death enacted than any other previous generation as a result of the wide, almost global, access to film and television.

A project organized by the research and pressure group Cultural Indicators in the USA estimated that the average American child sees 3,000 violent screen deaths by the age of twelve. That is before the age many children find approved access to 'adult' programming where violent death is a staple part of entertainment. Another estimate based on the American television industry puts the figure of screen deaths witnessed much higher. Although the figure is now twenty-five years old there is no reason to suppose that it has substantially changed. Andrew Quicke in *Tomorrow's Television* claimed the average American child at the age of fourteen had witnessed 18,000 people killed on-screen.[15]

Quicke also cites a monitoring of American television over a sample eight-hour period when ninety-three specific incidents of brutality and murder were noted. The death toll cited makes it sound as if James Bond films, complete with the hero's licence to kill, had been shown constantly. People had been shot, dropped in molten sugar, trussed, beaten by hoodlums, tortured over live coals and drowned.[16]

The British film critic Milton Shulman calculated that the average British boy spent one-seventh of his waking life encountering screen or other forms of fictional violence – and this was before the widespread availability of computer games. In these games watching violent death being enacted by others has been replaced by the viewer becoming an active participant. Success in the various militaristic computer games is achieved by killing the highest number of aliens or villains on-screen. The Movement for Christian Democracy published a report in 1999 which claimed that a quarter of British children were addicted to computer games, screen trivia and violence. Computer games with names such as *Panzer Commander*, *Duke Nukem*, *Total Annihilation*, *Dead or Alive* and *Crime Killer* were described as unrealistic, manipulative and dishonest.[17]

Screen deaths are, however, false deaths. Computer victims are clearly fantasy figures. When cowboys shoot Indians they fall cleanly and the camera seldom lingers on their death throes. If it does, as happens in certain gratuitously violent films, the technicolour gore remains two-dimensional. The smell of death cannot reach through the screen. The true fear of evil is not there because the viewer can always switch off the television set or leave the cinema.

That is not to say some sensitive or vulnerable viewers are not disturbed or damaged by what they see. In extreme cases that disturbance might manifest itself in the viewer becoming immune to the concept of violent death. As time passes, when war and disaster are reported on news programmes, these viewers do not feel sympathy, as they others might, for the real-life victims shown. That mental damage or desensitization is achieved without them experiencing the true nature of death.

Even deathbed scenes project a largely false image of death. Very few people in real life pass from lucidity to death peacefully in a matter of moments with the head sinking gently back onto a clean pillow. This, however, is often how deaths are portrayed on-screen. And if a death is not shown in this way, the chances are it is an unnatural one. Statistically screen deaths are overwhelmingly unnatural, with a highly disproportionate number of the fictional or dramatic deaths shown being murders.

Back in the real world, employing modern medical techniques, we can delay death more effectively than any generation has been able to do before us. In the Western world average life expectancy rose consistently in the twentieth century. Infant mortality, once a common and sad but accepted part of family life, is now rare. But we still do not know what happens after death, and most of us, for most of the time, prefer not to ask.

There have been many stories told about the afterlife. Heaven, hell, purgatory and reincarnation have all been featured. One has the impression that, in some cultures, belief in life beyond the grave has been so strong that people faced the prospect and process of death in a very matter-of-fact way, with about the same level of concern that we in the Western world might have in boarding a plane or train to go on an important journey to start a new chapter in life.

In societies bound together by common religious practices, which provided the underpinning explanation for the mysteries of existence – birth, illness, suffering and dying – death was often incorporated into a wider redemptive scheme. This was especially true in Christian societies where the passion, death and resurrection of Christ provided a secure foundation. The words from the Church of England's Book of Common Prayer, dating back over 400 years, express this well. At the graveside, as earth is cast upon the lowered coffin, the priest recites one of the most hauntingly familiar passages of English prose: 'earth to earth, ashes to ashes, dust to dust; in sure and certain hope of the Resurrection to eternal life, through our Lord Jesus Christ; who shall change our vile body, that it may be like unto his glorious body, according to the mighty working, whereby he is able to subdue all things to himself'.

It can be argued that our economically developed secular society has, in the main, abandoned its collective ability to see purpose in life and death, and only a few members still attempt to find any redemptive purpose. The nearest modern Western society comes to finding redemptive purpose in death is when, after an accident, there is a demand to find the cause. If a cause is found it is thought that the mistakes which resulted in the first death will not be repeated. If future lives can be saved, it is then said that the original death was not in vain.

A Christian will argue that the death of Jesus redeemed humankind and provided the promise of eternal life. Yet, conversely, it does not always follow that a person who claims that death has no redemptive purpose will also say that they do not believe in an afterlife – whatever form that afterlife might take. In what is described as the postmodern era, the public expression of a common set of beliefs and values – a Christian set in much of the Western world – has been replaced by every individual finding a belief system of their own which suits their own needs. Sometimes these individuals 'mix and match' selections of belief, which appear to Christians to be inconsistent.

In medieval Europe, everyone from priest to peasant, nobleman to nobody, would have shared a common vision of the afterlife which involved judgement, then punishment or reward – complete with fire, brimstone and demons in the one place and angels in the other. Interestingly, however, it was not until 1512 that the concept of the immortality of the individual human soul became an article of Catholic dogma.

Today a whole spectrum of possibilities is entertained, although hell and damnation do not figure highly. The 'hellfire and damnation' preachers are still at work, but it appears they no longer put the same fear of God into their congregations. This failure to instil fear is welcomed by some liberal theologians as a sign of spiritual maturity. Theologian Don Cupitt, for instance, makes this point. 'In modern times the fear of Hell has suddenly disappeared as a motive for living the Christian life,' he wrote in 1991. 'We no longer seem to need it. It seems that we are already making the transition to a more adult… religious outlook.'[18]

With or without damnation as a high-profile option, the modern spectrum, or range, of beliefs can be examined in two ways: firstly by survey and secondly by an analysis of expressions of popular sentiment. The first is a more scientific and controlled method of study and is the more objective approach. The second takes a more impressionistic and subjective approach. The first will be of greater statistical validity; the second will explore ideas in a more open-ended way and not be subject to the restrictions of categorization set by researchers and others.

Douglas Davies and Alastair Shaw, in their report on popular British attitudes to death published in 1995, identified five main categories of belief concerning an afterlife.

Respondents to their survey which involved a randomly selected sample of 736 men and 867 women from around Britain, were shown a card and asked, 'Which, if any, of the views on this card accord with your own attitude to life after death?'

1. Nothing happens, we come to the end of life.
2. Our soul passes to another world.
3. Our bodies await resurrection.
4. We come back as something or someone else.
5. Trust in God, all is in God's hands.[19]

Respondents were free to choose more than one option, but only 21 per cent did so. The majority selected a single category.

Just over a third of those interviewed felt that the soul passes after death to another world. By a small margin they outnumbered those who believed that death was the end of life. Almost 22 per cent said that they trusted in God and that what happened to them after death was in his hands. Reincarnation was considered by 12 per cent as the most likely outcome of death. Category 3, resurrection, was selected by only 8 per cent of respondents.

What comes as something of a surprise is the way in which these results tally with professed religious beliefs. While the sample interviewed was chosen at random, once selected, each respondent was asked to describe their religious affiliation, if any. As Douglas Davies pointed out in his commentary on the figures:

The idea of resurrection... played an extremely small part in people's responses with 4 per cent of Anglicans and 6 per cent of Church of Scotland members choosing it. No Methodists selected it at all. Only the Roman Catholics at 18 per cent gave any sort of indication of the possible importance of the doctrine. Given that it lies at the traditional heart of worship and theology in all these churches one might, perhaps, have expected to see the idea of resurrection being chosen more often by more of the churches' members.[20]

Each worshipping member of those churches, one might assume, would have been familiar with the declaration of faith in the concluding words of the creed as said collectively at the communion service: 'I look for the resurrection of the dead and the life of the world to come.'

However, reincarnation, a belief which has no place in Christian theology, was the option chosen by 14 per cent of Anglicans, 11 per cent of Roman Catholics and 6 per cent each of those from the Methodist Church and Church of Scotland. The poll was taken before the football coach and manager Glenn Hoddle made his much-publicized statement of belief in reincarnation in which he suggested that the law of karma operated, and that people who needed further testing in a future life might return with a disability. Hoddle's views were interpreted as so inappropriate and politically incorrect that he was forced into giving up his post with the England football team. As Douglas Davies observed, when reviewing the findings of his survey, 'It is obvious that from wider cultural ideas, the concept of returning as another entity appeals to people since this seems to be accepted at a higher level than the official idea of resurrection which is taught and expressed in many hymns and in the rites of the Easter festival.'[21]

The most curious finding of all is that 32 per cent of the polled Anglicans, 30 per cent of the Methodists, 22 per cent of Church of Scotland members and 14 per cent of Roman Catholics indicated that they believed that death was the end of life and nothing happened beyond the grave.

The second approach to studying current belief, that of examining expressions of popular sentiment, produces a rather different picture. Bereavement cards, designed to bring comfort and support to the relatives of those who have died, make no mention of death being the end, nor do they raise the possibility of reincarnation. Perhaps they are only marketed to those who opted for categories 2 or 5, although there is sufficient ambiguity in most examples for respondents to category 1 to find meaning in and to empathize with the words. In keeping with the postmodern age, the cards do not normally express a Christian viewpoint, but draw on familiar poems and passages of prose which have found their way into the standard bereavement repertoire.

In some instances the words are those of the departed comforting those who mourn, like these written originally by a Victorian canon of St Paul's Cathedral in London, Henry Scott Holland:

Death is nothing at all. I have only slipped away into the next room. I am I and you are you. Whatever we were to each other, that we still are. Call me by my old familiar names, speak to me in the easy ways you always used. Put no difference in your tone, wear no forced air of solemnity or sorrow. Laugh as we always laughed at the little jokes we enjoyed together. Play, smile, think of me, pray for me. Let my name be ever the household word that it always was, let it be spoken without effort, without the trace of a shadow on it. Life means all that it ever meant. It is the same as it ever was: there is unbroken continuity. Why should I be out of sight? I am waiting for you, for an interval, somewhere very near, just around the corner. All is well.[22]

The canon's words form the preface to the much-read secular guide to arranging a funeral produced by the multinational firm of funeral directors SCI and made widely available to their customers.[23]

A poll conducted to discover the 100 most popular poems of today was conducted in 1995 to coincide with the year's National Poetry Day. Several of the poems included on the list were on the subject of death. One, however, was not included, but got a special mention from the compilers of the list. It had arrived on the scene too late to be considered. It was a modern poem which had just become astonishingly popular. The secular funeral guide mentioned above, which starts with Canon Holland's words, ends with this modern poem. It was published anonymously and was said to have been written by a soldier serving in Northern Ireland, left in an envelope to be opened and read by his parents should he be killed:

Do not stand at my grave and weep;
I am not there. I do not sleep.
I am a thousand winds that blow,
I am the diamond glints on snow.
I am the sunlight on ripened grain,
I am the gentle autumn rain.
When you awaken in the morning hush
I am the swift uplifting rush
Of quiet birds in circled flight.
I am the soft stars that shine at night.
Do not stand at my grave and cry;
I am not there. I did not die.

Near the top of the list of 100 poems were these familiar words by Christina Rossetti from her poem 'Remember':

Remember me when I am gone away,
    Gone far away into the silent land;
    When you can no more hold me by the hand...
Yet if you should forget me for a while
    And afterwards remember, do not grieve:
    For if the darkness and corruption leave
    A vestige of the thoughts that once I had,
Better by far you should forget and smile
    Than that you should remember and be sad.[24]

When the film *Four Weddings and a Funeral* became an unexpected box-office hit, one of the offshoots of its success was the discovery for many cinema-goers of a poem by W.H. Auden.

It was recited by the gay lover of a man who had, in the fullness of life, been suddenly struck down by a heart attack.

'Stop all the clocks, cut off the telephone...' was how it started, and it ended with some poignant lines which spoke of the finality of death;

the stars were no longer wanted, the moon was to be packed up and the sun was to be dismantled.[25]

Those who see death as a finality see no ambiguity in Rossetti's words. The words of the unknown soldier, however, are open to wide interpretation. They could be telling of the mystical absorption of the soul into the love of God, or possibly foreshadowing nirvana, a state of wholeness in which the ego is no more. Rossetti's poem, however, is a plea to be remembered, but no statement of hope. It even suggests that once forgotten, best forgotten: the living should get on with life and leave the dead behind. W.H. Auden's words are those of an empty soul so consumed with grief that nothing will console. They are not unprecedented and strike a common chord with Christ's agonizing words at the moment of death on the cross, 'My God, my God, why has thou forsaken me?' except that the words of an atheist have a different kind of desolation. They do not even have a God to blame.

Another work by Christina Rossetti did not get into the top 100, but expresses many of the same sentiments as 'Remember', and has also been adopted as a popular verse for secular funerals:

> When I am dead, my dearest,
> Sing no sad songs for me;
> Plant thou no roses at my head,
> Nor shady cypress tree:
> Be the green grass above me,
> With showers and dewdrops wet;
> And if thou wilt, remember,
> And if thou wilt, forget.[26]

Written words of bereavement which are the spontaneous work of the grieving can be found on the handwritten cards left with flowers at gravesides or other places associated with death. Increasingly flowers are left by the roadside where a person has been killed in a car crash, or at a public site when a high-profile death occurs. Following the shooting of the schoolchildren at Dunblane in Scotland, in March 1996, thousands of bouquets of flowers were left outside the school, and at the time of the death of Diana, Princess of Wales, tens of thousands of bouquets were left in her memory and messages were left addressed to her. The messages expressed a blend of romanticism and Christian theology, sentimentality borrowing images from a theology which is anything but sentimental. The concepts of God and the images of the afterlife revealed in the thousands of letters and poems written, bore witness to one strand of the popular understanding of the divine shared by many people in Britain in the last decade of the twentieth century.

A collection of letters written by children and published as *Diana, Children's Letters to God* illustrated this well:

Dear God, Make sure she makes friends in heaven.

Dear God, Please look after a new angel in heaven.

Dear God, please keep her safe and let her rest with the angels.

Please look after the Queen of Hearts in heaven.

Dear God, Diana will always be the brightest star in the sky.[26]

From the many cards left at the royal palaces further examples of popular religious imagery were found: 'Dolphins have strength to be free, now you are free with Dodi in heaven.' This reference to dolphins can be attributed to the belief, held by many followers of New Age mystics, that dolphins have a highly developed gift of spiritual awareness from which healing can flow. Other messages were less New Age, but certainly the range could be described as postmodern in that it represented a diversity of spiritual images – some Christian and some only on the borderline of Christian orthodoxy:

You were the heart and soul of the country, your soul will live on in
our hearts forever.

You are safe now my little angel.

The good on earth are always snatched the earliest.

Thank you for the love you gave the poor, may the Lord make you
a saint.

Beautiful eternal princess of heaven.

Around the first anniversary of the death of the princess more
messages were left, although not in such numbers. The emphasis had,
however, changed and Diana was seen not as someone being received
into heaven, but as someone who could mediate from beyond.

At the Place D'Alma, which stands above the subway where Diana
was fatally injured, there is a sculpture of a golden flame which has been
adopted as an unofficial Diana shrine. In August 1998 it was covered
with messages. Many of them were expressed in the language normally
associated with pious Catholic devotion to Mary. Diana was described
as Queen of Heaven. There were requests for her prayers and for her
to intervene to heal sickness.

Two years after her death many of the thousands of messages left at
prominent sites in London contained a demand for a permanent
memorial to the princess to be set up. The memorial presumably would
act as the official shrine in much the same way as the Place D'Alma and
Kensington Palace gates serve as unofficial shrines at present. There
was evidence, too, of individuals setting up their own shrines in their
own homes. One message left at Kensington came from a girl who
signed herself Simone. 'I am nine. I have my bedroom wall covered in
pictures of you.' Religious shrines often use candles and perfume to
create the right atmosphere of tranquillity and devotion and scented

Diana candles have been manufactured and sold by the thousand. The best-known unofficial memorial to the princess and Dodi Fayed, who was in the car with Diana and also died, is to be found at Harrod's, the London store owned by Dodi's father. Other messages left in London spoke of Diana's perpetual presence in words as if written by the princess herself:

I did not leave you at all. I am still with you. I am in the sun and in the wind. I am even in the rain. I did not die, I am with you all.

To the valley of your mind let me arrive. I did not die and am still alive.

In both examples, the style is reminiscent of the unknown soldier's poem. It is as if the departed is speaking from beyond the grave.

One of the most curious and disturbing of the messages had apocalyptic overtones. It read like a prophecy of the end of the world, the punishment of wrongdoers and the return of Christ: 'I'll see you again when the stars fall from the sky, and the moon turns red over this green Earth.'

The only similar collection of popular and spontaneous expressions of visions of an afterlife relating to the death of a twentieth-century figure is that connected with Elvis Presley. Poetry is published in fan magazines and the stone wall which fronts Presley's home and burial place at Graceland in Memphis, Tennessee, is covered in messages and prayers. Visitors to Graceland almost feel obliged to leave their mark on the wall which is some 300 yards long, five feet tall and covered in writing. Every few months the writing is sandblasted away and within weeks the empty space is filled again:

We lost a King, but heaven has gained one.

To the King. I will love you forever. We will meet again.

Mansions in heaven. I see myself walking with the King. The angels are descending to carry me up.

This verse is from a British Elvis fan magazine:

> For death is not goodbye
> for we all meet again
> to share eternal youth
> on some Nebula plain.

As is this:

> If there is a heaven
> And a God whose love is true.
> Then I am sure, Elvis,
> God now lives alongside you.

In the case of Diana, the sentiments expressed were not universally acclaimed and some people felt impelled to dissociate themselves from what they perceived as gross and erroneous sentimentality. 'The tributes were heartfelt and passionately sincere,' wrote Jeremy Seabrook in the January 1998 edition of *Resurgence*:

> But in a society where the sense of religion has decayed, the reaching for transcendence in often banal. 'Your body crucified like that of Christ,' said one card. 'Guide us eternally from above,' besought another. The messages showed that people still believe in an infantile heaven – 'Dodi and Diana together in paradise.' 'In heaven you will have privacy and peace at last.'… This was a mixture of fairy tale and folk-religion: a faith for the consumer society.[28]

Away from the extraordinary and unique Diana context, the more everyday written expressions of grief share much of what Seabrook would identify as the infantile. It is easy to scoff at some of the verse as naïve or banal, and an epitaph written for a little girl buried in an Australian cemetery is said to read as follows:

> She was our flower, but you Lord have taken our little Nell,
> To be in heaven with you, to enjoy her smell.

While these two lines are in all probability apocryphal, a glance through the *in memoriam* columns of any local newspaper will provide examples of verse which sophisticates would mock. These examples come from the both the far North and the South-East of Britain:

> Time cannot dim the face I love,
> The voice I heard each day,
> The many things he did for me,
> In his own loving way.
> I cannot bring the old days back,
> His hand I cannot touch,
> But I'll never lose the memory
> Of the one I loved so much.

> A heart of gold stopped beating,
> Two smiling eyes at rest,
> God broke our hearts to prove us.
> He only takes the best.

> They say there is a reason,
> They say time will heal,
> But neither time nor reason
> Will change the way I feel.

> Two tired eyes are sleeping,
> Two willing hands are still,
> The one who worked so hard for us,
> Is sleeping at God's will.

It would be wrong and intellectually arrogant, however, for such lines to be dismissed as unworthy of attention, for they are sincere and revealing. The general thrust of the messages mourners choose to leave as handwritten notes, and the sentiments they buy as printed off-the-shelf expressions of grief or hope reveal theologies of two sorts. First of all they reveal a belief that God may and does take away that which he has created. It is his prerogative as creator to take his creatures unto himself. In this context, death is not regarded as simply the product of accident, misfortune, old age, self-abuse or disease. Death happens to people whom God has chosen and their deaths happen at a time of God's choosing. One popular saying used when someone dies young goes like this, 'God must have loved her very much to have wanted her with him.' It is a theology that suggests three ideas which are not orthodox to any major religion: firstly, that to be with God a person has to be in heaven, implying that God is not present here on earth; secondly, that God is selfish and takes people away from their friends and families for his own pleasure; and thirdly, that people are essentially immortal, but that immortality is a gift of, and thus at the beck and call of, a higher being. That higher being, however, that God, is not regarded as vengeful in popular folk-faith. He is not feared as the jealous God of the Old Testament. What he does, and who he takes, he does in love for a higher purpose.

And that acceptance leads on to another point which emerges from the written evidence. It is the idea that those whom God takes to himself, he protects until such time as they may be reunited with those they loved, but have left behind. 'Do not speak ill of the dead,' is a commonly used phrase, and in writing of the dead it is a common assumption that the departed are winging their way to a protective paradise and that sometime in the future they will be reunited with the living.

In terms of Douglas Davies' five categories, the written evidence suggests that a notion of resurrection exists. It is implicit that the soul must have life again if a reunion with loved ones is to occur. The departed may rest in peace for now, but in order to meet again with those they loved on earth, they must surely rise again. The idea that God is in charge, and to be trusted, figures very strongly in the written evidence, as does the belief in another place to which the soul will go. Reincarnation gets no mention at all, which runs counter to the evidence of the survey, and nihilism is only represented by those verses which are so unspecific that they could embrace any possibility. This verse came from a local Kent newspaper paid entry – a common practice that entails the bereaved buying space in which to publish their poems and tributes:

> For no one knows the heartache that lies behind our smiles,
> No one knows how many times we've broken down and cried.
> We want to tell you something, so there's no doubt,
> You are so wonderful to think of,
> But so hard to live without.

Combining the poll findings with the written material, no clear picture emerges of contemporary belief. It is fragmented and eclectic. All five main categories find supporters and no single category dominates. What is not revealed by either approach to the subject, neither the study of the poll nor the study of writings, is the intensity of belief. Did respondents to the poll who said they believed in reincarnation, for instance, truly believe that they would return in another form, or only half believe? Do people who write of meeting again in heaven sincerely believe that will happen, or are they merely finding temporary respite from grief in sentimental poetry?

It might be supposed that those who took the trouble to express their ideas in writing had taken more time and thought over expressing their views than those selected randomly to take part in an opinion poll. Furthermore, those who took pen in hand might have felt themselves less restrained in what they said. Without an interviewer sitting beside them, ready, so the respondent might fear, to judge them by their answers, the writers' imaginations could take over. But imaginations have to be fuelled with stories and images. Few have the gift of true creativity and while the interviewer could help people best express their feelings by presenting them with multiple-choice questions, the writers were restricted in the images they chose. While 'love', 'heaven', 'God' or 'angels' were words they knew and could use, did they truly know what those words signify? Can anyone know?

Many of the messages left for Diana were written on home-made cards. The cards were made from pictures of the princess cut from newspapers and magazines. Often the cards were heart-shaped and adorned with paper roses. Sometimes cut-out paper angels were incorporated in the designs. In much the same way that the words used had been recycled for a new purpose, so had the visual images. In the process the original meanings of both words and images were changed to suit their new purpose. In a floral tribute to Diana displayed as part of a flower festival in a Kent church,[29] a playing card of the Queen of Hearts was given pride of place.

One is left with the conclusion that in their own words and through their own handmade artwork many people are struggling to express transcendent ideas, but they are not always successful. They seldom have the means or language to satisfactorily convey these ideas to others. From this modern-day folk-art only a vague idea can be gathered by others of what people believe when they are talking of things beyond this world and beyond their understanding. Perhaps one has to examine what people do when faced with death to get a clearer picture. This can be done from two perspectives: that of the person who is dying and knows the end is close, and that of the onlookers who remain behind once death has taken its course.

CHAPTER FOUR

Where is the Evidence?

There would be conclusive proof of life after death if contact could be made by the living with the dead and that contact could be proven to be genuine. Furthermore if the message from beyond the grave was comforting and reassuring as well as believable, the natural fear of death would be removed. Similarly, if people could, in some way, during their life here on earth, receive a foretaste of the afterlife, they would then be reassured that death was not the end. Yet again, if reincarnation is to be our destiny, it would be all the more plausible if we could each, in some way, recall past lives and check our recollections against historical evidence.

Some individuals do claim that they have been shown the afterlife. Several visionaries have talked of the privilege of being given glimpses of heaven. John the Divine's book of Revelation is the most celebrated account. Also in the Bible, there is the far earlier account of Jacob dreaming of a ladder joining earth and heaven on which he saw angels ascending and descending.[1]

Visionaries today, like Christina Gallagher in Ireland, continue to claim visions from beyond the grave. Gallagher is also a stigmatic and sometimes displays wounds on her body corresponding to the marks of

Christ's passion and crucifixion. Her most graphic descriptions are those of hell and purgatory. Gallagher describes how she has witnessed the suffering of souls beyond death and warns of the punishment that is to come to all who do not turn away from sin. Her descriptions of souls suffering in purgatory are gruesomely vivid and involve all the fire and brimstone imagery made popular by the medieval church: 'Then I could see people running out of the fire and they were on fire. I could see the area of fire being surrounded by devils.'[2]

Within the Eastern non-Christian traditions there are descriptions to be found of the afterlife recounted by those who are said to have been to other worlds and 'returned'. *The Tibetan Book of the Dead* is said to be the work of reincarnated lamas, holy men, who have written of their previous lives and the time spent between. They recounted how there were many bright lights and fearful sounds, and their descriptions are not dissimilar to those of visionaries from other faith traditions, and in particular those who report near-death experiences.

The sensation of being out of the body in some way and being drawn towards lights and sounds is widely reported. It is frequently interpreted by those who have the sensation as being a glimpse of the afterlife and is, by a long way, the most common form that a supposed glimpse of the afterlife takes. A 1982 Gallup poll conducted in the USA suggested that 8 million Americans had had such an experience.

Also widely reported are the accounts given by patients who are revived after they have passed a point of what would, at one time, have been irreversible death. The sensations, sights and sounds they report are remarkably consistent with each other and with other out-of-body experiences. Frequently these patients report a feeling of being lifted out of their bodies. They say that they see themselves as dispassionate outside observers. Then they are drawn into a tunnel at the end of which is a bright light. During this time they find that their existence takes on a whole new perspective. In some instances patients find their past life laid out before them, or it is flashed before their eyes. They feel calm and ready to be absorbed into the light, but, as their physical bodies are revived, they are suddenly returned to the world. They almost always describe how reluctant they are to return. Some say that on their return they have a mission to fulfil. Almost invariably they say, from the time of the experience onwards, they have no fear of dying.

Occasionally negative near-death experiences are reported. One Christian cardiologist reports that one fifth of the patients he has revived after their hearts have stopped, and who describe visions of an afterlife, describe going to a hell-like state. One woman told him how she entered a gloomy room and saw imps, elves and a giant. She was impelled to go outside into the darkness with the giant. She could hear people moaning all around her. She was dragged into a dark tunnel, but suddenly the giant let her loose and she returned to life with a great feeling of relief that she had been spared a ghastly fate.[3]

A near-death experience is not something reported by everyone who undergoes the first stages of death. A man I once met who had been clinically dead for twenty minutes, having been pulled lifeless from water, told me with some disappointment that he had had no strange or ethereal experience – simply no recollection of anything. What might explain the accounts of those who do report the classic symptoms of a near-death experience? Have they truly had a glimpse of heaven? Might they, conversely, be describing nothing more than a hallucination brought about by the process of dying as the body becomes starved of oxygen and endorphins are released. Dr Susan Blackmore, one of many academics who have studied the subject, endorses this functional view. As the retina at the back of the eye ceases to receive the oxygen supply it needs, it is believed that the nerve cells start to fire at random. Where there is a particular concentration of nerve cells a bright spot is seen which resembles the end of a tunnel. Dr Blackmore does not believe in an afterlife herself, yet she concludes that in the near-death experience the dying person has a sense of profound enlightenment. They believe that they have acquired a sense of realization of the truth, but what in reality is happening, she believes, is nothing to do with divine love or wisdom.

They are experiencing a subjective illusion of insight brought about by the breakdown of the model of self which results from the collapse of the brain's normal processes:

> It can cut right through the illusion that we are separate selves. It becomes obvious that 'I' never did exist and so there is no one to die. The funny thing is that when a whole system drops the idea of there being anyone to die, it seems to become a nicer person to have around. To the extent that it happens, the person is changed. Here is the real loss of the fear of death. Here lies the true transformation of the experience.[4]

Carl Jung, when unconscious after a heart attack in 1944, had a vision of being taken out of himself and away from the earth. His reflection on the experience is not dissimilar to that of Susan Blackmore in that he felt his notion of self being challenged. 'Everything I had aimed at or wished for or thought, the whole phantasmagoria of earthly existence, fell away or was stripped from me – an extremely painful process. Nevertheless something remained; it was as if I now carried along with me everything I had ever experienced or done… I consisted of my own history, and I felt with great certainty: this is what I am.'[5]

Experiences of the near-death kind have been recreated using volunteers taking hallucinogenic drugs. They have also been reported by people who have suffered no physical harm, but who are expecting to die at any moment. Parachutists whose parachutes have failed to open and rock-climbers who have fallen from mountainsides, and who have amazingly lived to tell the tale, have sometimes been able to recall a sense of heightened awareness akin to a near-death experience before hitting the ground. There is certainly evidence drawn from victims of trauma and war that when near to death the body's own natural sedatives, endorphins, are released and victims remain calm and pain-free despite horrendous injuries. Perhaps also the shock of expecting to die produces the same effect.

Whatever the explanation, the experience is described by those who have been through it as a spiritual one. They identify the light with God. On their return to earthly life they want to share the insights they have had with others. In one case a Texan, Robert Campbell, who had a vision closely resembling a near-death experience, was returned to consciousness convinced that he had the duty to tell the world that he had discovered the true identity of the Messiah – not Jesus, but Elvis Presley! 'There was a blinding, or almost blinding white light and a voice like thunder came from out of the light, "Go back and tell them: Elvis." It was the voice of God. And in an instant I was back in the chair where I had been sitting.' Robert Campbell described how he had not wanted to return to his life as the light was so compelling and loving, and that he had had the temerity to argue with God, but to no avail.[6]

While a near-death experience provides powerful proof of life beyond this world to those who have first-hand knowledge of one, it is a subjective experience and no objective endorsement of it can be made. There is also no way of knowing what might have happened if the experience had continued; would it have lasted for eternity, or would it have petered out into oblivion? Without that knowledge there is no way of disproving Susan Blackmore and others who say that the experience is part of the dying process. In that sense it fails as an objective proof of life after death. No one can accompany another on a near-death experience and come back to give testimony that what that person believed happened to them did in fact happen.

Attached to the story of Jung's sickbed vision is a curious addendum. In Stuart Gordon's comprehensive review of the near-death-experience phenomenon he notes an account that Jung's nurse later gave of the moment from her perspective. She said that as the celebrated psychologist lay seemingly oblivious to his material surroundings at the time of his vision, 'He had been surrounded by a bright glow; something she had often witnessed in the dying'.[7] Stuart Gordon concludes that near-death experiences strongly suggest that consciousness can exist independently of time, space and matter. The experiences, therefore, support the notion of the existence of an immaterial element – soul or spirit – that invigorates the body when associated with it. 'That the experiences occur is as undeniable as the evidence that those experiencing them find their outlook on life changed as a result.'[8]

There now exists an International Association for Near-Death Studies. It is chaired by David Lorimer who, in 1998, addressed a conference on death organized by the Findhorn Community. The Community, based in Scotland, teaches no specific religious code, but is a gathering place for a variety of students of religion – mostly New Age, but including some Christians.

David Lorimer talked of people who had undergone near-death experiences as gaining a new appreciation of life. He described how people find themselves reorientated after they have had the experience, with changed priorities and values. Typically they would go from an attitude where having material possessions was most important to one where being and inner connectedness, and the search for love and wisdom, had become the most important things in their lives. As David Lorimer put it, 'the ultimate take-home message' of the near-death experience is that life is about growing in wisdom and in our capacity for love.[9]

What is remarkable about near-death experiences as reported is their consistency. In one famous study of the phenomenon, fifteen separate elements were reported to recur again and again. Although the different elements attracted different descriptions according to culture – for instance Christians talked of being drawn towards Christ while Jews talked of approaching angels – the core experience remained constant. The transcending of cultures was confirmed when Susan Blackmore interviewed nineteen people from the Indian subcontinent who had been returned from death, their descriptions differing little from those given by Westerners. 'The stages of the tunnel are very likely to be universal,' David Lorimer concurs. 'They symbolize the passage from one type of reality to another. The experience is saying that consciousness can exist apart from the physical brain.'[10]

In some of the Eastern religious traditions, scholars and mystics have made detailed studies of the metaphysics of the dying process which suggest that the near-death experience is part of a wider and more subtle experience. As the Dalai Lama wrote,

> A person who dies naturally within physical well-being and without much physical deterioration will remain in the state of the subtlest mind, the mind of clear light, for about three days. When within that subtle mind of clear light there is a very slight movement, the mind of clear light ceases, the consciousness exits from the old body and you begin the reverse process, going back into the mind of radiant black near-attainment and the other six levels of appearance – radiant red appearance, radiant white appearance, appearance like a burning butter lamp, appearance like fireflies, appearance like smoke and appearance like a mirage.[11]

The reverse process concludes in rebirth, so the Dalai Lama's tradition teaches. There is certainly an almost universal belief in the existence of a soul which can exist outside the body. Going back as far as the beliefs of the ancient Egyptians one finds reference to the soul flying above the body and leaving the earth. In many cultures there are specific descriptions of how the soul departs through the nostrils or mouth. It is as if the breath of life itself is leaving, the opposite process to that described in Genesis when the breath of God entered the clay, the dead matter, to create human life.[12]

Before leaving the subject of near-death experiences, mention should be made of out-of-body experiences which are not associated with dying. One example is given in a description by an Australian professor of what he felt happening to him as he lay in a hospital bed in Thailand. He had been taken to hospital after eating a poisoned, or drugged, sweet. He said that he simply entered a timeless space void. He felt totally alive in an almost palpable blackness which was somehow radiant. It was a sensation so beyond his experience that he could only describe it by borrowing lines from a poem by Henry Vaughan called 'The Night': 'There is in God (some say) a deep but dazzling darkness.'[13]

Interestingly Christina Gallagher describes visions of heaven which closely resemble near-death experiences, but which have come to her in a trance-like state:

> Our Holy Mother came to me and said, 'Come my child, come,' and I could see myself running towards her. Then Our Holy Mother put steps of light in front of me and I ran up the steps. The warmth I felt as she drew me to her heart! I felt myself sinking into her Heart… Then I could see the most strong light. Then the light formed a sky and ground and all upwards and then falling down. It was like diamonds sparkling.[14]

Bilocation, the ability to be in two places at the same time, is another form of out-of-body experience and has been connected with several holy or saintly people. Many stories are told of the Italian friar Padre Pio achieving this feat, although the stories have tended to grow in the telling and the original facts are now impossible to establish. Bilocation is not confined to saints and I have a friend who has described a sensation to me which he says has come to him on several occasions: 'At certain times I have had this weird experience. I have found myself miles away next to a friend of mine to whom I turn at times of crisis. Later she tells me how she too felt my presence close to her at the time.'[15]

Out-of-body experiences have been achieved, so it is reported, during yogic meditation. *The Tibetan Book of the Dead* describes how an ethereal duplicate of the physical body exists which can travel. Some New Age cults and traditional shamans believe in astral travel – an ability, so it is said, for the personality to travel across space in an ethereal form. For this to happen, according to standard descriptions, a second subtle body becomes the vehicle of travel. *The Encyclopedia of Mystical and Paranormal Experience* describes the body as a ghostly, semi-transparent double of the physical body. To other individuals it is said to be invisible, although its presence may be sensed. Sometimes the vehicle of astral travel is not a ghostly body, but a point of light or concentration of energy. In some instances astral travellers are said to be aware of a silvery cord connecting their ethereal self to their physical self.

In the astral form the traveller moves at the speed of thought and can travel through solid objects on the earthly plane, as well as entering a new realm described as the astral plane. Travellers report leaving and re-entering their physical bodies through the head or solar plexus, and they belive that if the silver cord of a traveller is severed while he or she is outside the physical body then physical death occurs. The cord is said to break when the body dies and the consciousness or soul is released.

Reports of astral travel occur in many traditions. Surveys in the West suggest that around 25 per cent of people have had out-of-body experiences. One survey found that with marijuana users the figure rises to 44 per cent. The sensation may occur spontaneously or be induced by taking drugs or employing specific meditation techniques. Astral travel may be explained as hallucination or a dream. It is a subjective experience and one which cannot be scientifically verified. It provides, however, a very specific and common description of the potential for consciousness to exist outside the body. If astral travel occurs, and it is a big 'if', then it would propose the means by which the soul leaves on its journey from this life to the next. It would suggest that spirits are capable of travelling the world unseen. One must hope it is only a temporary state. To remain earthbound, seeing and hearing one's family and friends, but being unable to communicate with them, sounds a most distressing state of affairs. Astral travel, as a description of the interface between body and spirit, is not consistent with reports of near-death experiences. Does the soul leave the body and break the silver cord at the moment of physical death, or does the soul enter a long tunnel at the end of which is a beckoning and loving source of light?

Near-death experiences are believed by some researchers to be related to other curious phenomena, including reports of being abducted by aliens and the various forms of out-of-body sensation. What lies at the root of these various phenomena, it is said, is an electrochemical disturbance of the brain's temporal lobe. The main advocate of this line of thinking is a neurophysiologist from Laurentian University, Saskatchewan, Canada, Michael Persinger. He has described how micro-seizures of the temporal lobe might cause people to have hallucinations and believe they are undergoing paranormal experiences. He devised an experiment in which the temporal lobe is deliberately stimulated by electrical impulses, and subjects have reported visual, tactile and aural hallucinations. Dr Susan Blackmore, who volunteered as a subject, described the sensation: 'I was wide awake throughout... then suddenly my doubts vanished and I began swaying... then I felt as if two hands had grabbed my shoulders..., something seemed to get hold of my leg... then came the emotions. Out of the blue I suddenly felt angry... the feeling was replaced by an equally sudden attack of fear. I was terrified – of nothing in particular.'[16]

While out-of-body experiences and near-death experiences tell us nothing about what happens in the long term after death, accounts of such experiences, as consistent and numerous as they are, might be said to strongly suggest that the body and the soul can take on a separated existence. From that suggestion it might be thought to follow that the soul can survive eternally away from the body, when the day comes for the body to die. The logic is not watertight, but the sequence of the argument makes a strong case.

Establishing reincarnation as proof of life after death has been attempted using regressive hypnosis. Guided by the hypnotist, subjects are taken back through their lives, to their birth and then beyond, in an attempt to discover who they might once have been. Problems arise, however, when the details given of past lives are checked out. The details are normally far too unspecific to correlate with historical records. Thus those wishing to believe can find it easy to do so and sceptics can dismiss the notion with similar ease. Psychotherapists who believe that past lives can sometimes be recalled, claim that by identifying traumatic memories from past lives, explanations for current problems can be identified and the problems, whether mystery pains or phobias, can be faced. It is of interest to note that during hypnotic regression many subjects have reported a sensation of floating above their body as they relived their past. Some also describe contacting their 'inner wisdom' during these sessions and find that their view of life is changed as if by a spiritual experience.

In some very rare cases individuals, often children, describe a past life without the aid of hypnosis. Sometimes the incidents and places described are reported to match historical fact. This process of matching, however, needs to be carried out under rigorous scientific control to provide a convincing case. And even if details described match history well, reincarnation is just one of several explanations. Others might include the suggestion that the person recalling incidents is tapping into a collective memory, or has made some kind of telepathic link with a living person in possession of facts unknown to them, or that the recaller has somehow inadvertently and unknowingly absorbed facts about the past which they would not normally be expected to be able to do.

Some cultures accept stories of reincarnation more readily than others. There is a toddler in Sri Lanka who is widely claimed to be the reincarnation of the country's president Ranasinghe Premadasa, who was assassinated at a May Day rally in 1993. Even though the little boy, Sampath Wijebahu, lives in a remote village, a constant stream of visitors comes to the family home to see him. He is said to have correctly named the late president's wife and children and began to rise at three o'clock every morning to pray, a practice which the president had followed. When a researcher took the boy to the place where the president had been killed he began to cry, although, it was pointed out, this might have been because he had been taken away from his mother.

Sri Lanka claims many such cases. Nearer Europe, stories of reincarnation are given less credibility, although the story of an Irish mother coming back as the Englishwoman Jenny Cockell has been widely published. She believes that prior to her present life she was an Irish woman. She described in detail the village from which she had come and discovered a place in Ireland corresponding to her description. She also believes she has found the family she left behind when she died. She has had meetings with several adults she believes are her children from a previous existence.[17]

More generally reincarnation is said to account for birthmarks and soulmates. Birthmarks are supposedly scars left over from the wounds received in the course of a former existence. Soulmates are two people, who become great friends, dependent emotionally on each other and often inseparable, about whom it is said that they were partners in some former existence.

As unproven as reincarnation might seem to the sceptics of the Western world, it remains a widespread global belief. Hindus and Buddhists and many other historic faiths describe time as a cycle of birth and rebirth. That cycle is directed at a purpose which is the ultimate absorption of the soul, or personality, into something greater that transcends the individual. How this final outcome is described differs from one faith to another, but the ultimate notion of the overcoming of self is universal. 'Birth and death are part of the flow of things,' wrote Swami Bhavyananda giving a Hindu perspective:

> The individual soul, even before it reaches the human body, has assumed other bodies and cast them off. At the human level itself, the divine, though it has reached a level of self-consciousness, is still far away from manifestation... At one end of this voyage of discovery man is very nearly an animal; at the other end he is a saint, very nearly a God... Every lifetime is an opportunity to increase the manifestation of God-consciousness.[18]

While several Christian breakaway movements have embraced rein-carnation as a philosophy, no mainstream Christian church has ever taught it, although in the gospel accounts of John the Baptist, Jesus does appear to suggest that John was a reincarnated Elijah who had come to herald his arrival.[19]

Despite this general lack of support from the Christian theological tradition, reincarnation is a popular minority view in the West. A 1981 Gallup poll conducted in the USA found that 23 per cent of the adult population endorsed the idea. This figure included a high percentage of those who described themselves as members of one of the main Christian denominations. One illustration of this curious juxtaposition of ideas comes from the life of Diana, Princess of Wales. She expressed her belief in reincarnation in a conversation with a Church of England bishop at a private reception. She is reported to have told friends that her views left the bishop dumbfounded.

When it comes to the living having contact with others who are dead, there are several ways by which people believe they can bring this about. They include clairvoyance and spiritualism on the one hand, and the intervention of the saints on the other. Again, the problem persists in that these beliefs resist objective analysis and consequently fail to provide a level of proof of authenticity which could be widely accepted. Those who claim that it is possible to liaise with the dead talk of there being a thin veil separating this world from the next. The dead, they say, are there to be seen and heard on the 'other side', but the veil must be viewed in the right way if it is to be seen through. While everyone has the potential to see through the veil, it is said, only a few recognize that ability in themselves and can use it. Often a medium is required to help make the contact.

Mediumship is an ancient practice. It is defined as communication with alleged non-physical entities. Most cultures, including those of the developed Western world today, have included a strand of mediumship. It is an ancient and universal practice, the purpose of which is to facilitate divination, prophecy and conversation with the dead. Those who practise the 'art' have been known by many names. These include 'oracle, soothsayer, wizard, cunning or wise woman, witch, mystic, channeller and shaman'.[20] In some parts of the world, these shaman, or holders of wisdom, live divorced from the main community in order to devote their lives to the spiritual path. Some mediums claim to have spiritual guides to act as their agents in the world beyond.

In Britain and America mediumship is often a branch of showmanship. Public personalities like Doris Stokes hired theatres and took questions from their audiences. Deliberate charlatanism exists; so do mediums who genuinely believe in what they do and do not consciously practise any trickery. However, according to the scientist William Crookes who investigated 100 practitioners, all, in his opinion, resorted to trickery at times. The boundary between trickery and showmanship is narrow. Is the preacher who knows how to pace and present his sermon to the maximum effect employing tricks, or just being professional? When does 'gamesmanship' become 'trickery'?

Spiritualist churches have been set up in most major urban centres in Britain and attract regular and loyal congregations who meet for acts of worship which are followed by demonstrations of mediumship. Members of spiritualist churches tend to be older rather than younger and their numbers are diminishing. In the United Kingdom in 1975 the combined membership of the three main groups was estimated to be almost 57,000. The estimated figure for the year 2000 is 40,000. That decline is not necessarily a measure of a move away from a belief in spiritualism. It may be that it reflects the evolution of new forms of practising spiritualism. There is much anecdotal evidence to suggest that the various forms of New Age soothsaying, such as tarot readings, are on the increase.

Combined with a belief that it is possible to see into the world of the dead, is the belief that it is possible to see into the future. Michael Bentine, the comedian, was a lifelong believer in spiritualism, and wrote extensively on the subject. He told of this wartime experience when he was in the RAF. He described how before every bombing raid he would have a premonition as to which aircrew members would not survive the night:

Not just which member of a crew would go missing or parachute down to be captured, but actually which ones would die. I had an objective clairvoyant vision in which the face of the person I was looking at would change into a skull, as though I was suddenly looking through his skin and facial muscles. This dreadful experience was a hundred per cent accurate… I went to our experienced chaplain and told him what had happened. He didn't seem to be surprised and at his suggestion we knelt down together and prayed. Thank God the visions stopped. Then he told me I wasn't the only one who had suffered from that disturbing phenomenon.[21]

Some Christians would read into Bentine's account a demonic explanation. Others would say that he was suffering from stress hallucinations which he interpreted with hindsight as an accurate prediction of death. His account is of interest as an example of clairvoyance as it is perceived, but still does not provide the incontrovertible proof required for a supernatural phenomenon. That is not to doubt Bentine as an honest witness; it is to question his interpretation of his subjective experience. To Bentine, however, the disturbing episode fitted into his well-entrenched framework of life. He was the son of two keen and active spiritualists and had been brought up to accept that contact with the dead was not only possible, but also normal.

The dead, it is widely believed, can be contacted in several ways:

There is *clairvoyance* when a dead person, or something associated with that person, is seen. The vision might be in the mind's eye, in a dream, some ethereal form or in a form indistinguishable from the material world.

Then there is *clairaudience* when it is claimed that a sound or a voice is heard from beyond the grave. Frequently it is reported as a warning. Hearing voices is a subjective experience unique to the hearer and is frequently associated with mental illness. Nevertheless there are mediums who lay great store by their 'ability' to hear messages from the spirit world.

Psychometry is a development of the above using the sense of touch. Practitioners claim that by holding an object once owned or handled by a dead person they can divine information from it.

The above categories can be grouped together under the heading *clairsentience*. Whatever form clairsentience might take, it is described as a psychic ability. It can be inherited or learned, so it is claimed. It need not, however, involve contact with the world of the dead. It can be used to diagnose illness, travel distances within the current time frame or shape the content of dreams. Spiritual clairsentience is a subcategory which involves contact with, or visions of, a different or 'higher' plane of reality and angelic beings. Often practitioners of clairsentience need a catalyst or focus to aid them, such as a crystal ball or tarot cards. It is also said that they need to practise and hone their skills through meditative and spiritual exercises. It is a whole field of study and practice which, to the outsider, seems full of hocus-pocus and superstition. Because it is dealing with the unknown it is described as occult. Many people drawn into it become disturbed and frightened by it. There are several different types of contact that it is claimed can be made from beyond the grave:

Direct-voice contact is a form of mediumship involving the medium going into a trance and appearing to be another person. Their voice changes and the words they utter are said to be those of the spirit, entity or absent soul making contact with the listeners, who in turn may ask questions. In his public meetings at which he claims the Matreiya or new messiah is present, Benjamin Creme, a modern-day British religious leader, appears to go into a trance and speak as if through another personality.

Materialization is a form of contact with the dead which, in the past, has been frequently unmasked as fraudulent. Seances in which materialization happens are normally conducted in the dark and it is claimed ectoplasm, a strange pliable substance partly of and partly not of this world, oozes from the medium's body and takes on a significant shape.

Transfiguration is a rare form of mediumship which involves the superimposition of an alleged spirit face on that of the person conducting a seance.

Levitation and *telekinesis* are two further claimed manifestations of contact with the dead. It is said that the dead have the power to move or lift objects. They can make knocking sounds, move the glass of a ouija board or even raise and turn a table.

Automatic writing is when a medium records the messages from 'beyond' on paper, often at speed and in a handwriting not seemingly their own.

And finally, there are *apports*. These are physical objects which are said to manifest themselves. The Indian guru Sai Baba specializes in producing a spiritual dust to convince his followers of his powers. The Lincolnshire stigmatic Heather Woods once claimed that she had been given herbs from first-century Palestine in a vision and found them physically present when she awoke. She was, however, unable to find them when asked later for them to be studied.

Is contact truly made with the dead in the way that many people believe it to be? Many Christians will argue that the various manifestations outlined above are the work of evil and demonic powers. They will say that Satan, as the great deceiver, revels in creating havoc and delusion. Such practices as divination and clairvoyance, they will say, are forbidden in scripture and should play no part in Christian life.

The Bible gives many accounts of how God's power defeated the supposed power of magicians, and contains several outright condemnations of divination in its various forms: 'You shall not allow a witch to live,'[22] the children of Israel were told. 'Do not resort to ghosts and spirits, nor make yourselves unclean by seeking them out.'[23] 'Many of those who had become believers', it is said in the New Testament, 'came and openly confessed that they had been using magical spells. And a good many of those who had formerly practised magic collected their books and burnt them publicly.'[24]

There will be many today who take a scientific approach to the subject and condemn divination not for being contrary to the teaching of God, but as a form of self-deception which might lead to distress and fear. They will concede that contacts with the dead may be very real to those who wish to believe, or who are gullible and suggestible, or prone to hallucination, but that they are products of deception, a confused mind or the misinterpretation of evidence.

Of these three possibilities the last, misinterpretation of evidence, has most recently been investigated by Richard Wiseman of the Perrott Warwick Research Unit at the University of Hertfordshire. He arranged several experiments to demonstrate how, under conditions which recreated those of a seance, most people can misinterpret the evidence of their senses and thereby give themselves a misleading account of what in reality took place. The suggestibility of the mind allows for an illusion of the supernatural to be mistaken for the real thing.

Wiseman organized reconstructions of seances using the traditional techniques employed by mediums. In particular, participants sat in dimmed light around a table. To test the accuracy of voluntary participants' perceptions and recall of the sessions he conducted during the Fortean Times Unconvention, 1999, he asked them to fill in a questionnaire afterwards. A third of the sitters felt that they had or might have witnessed genuine unexplained phenomena involving visits from the spirit world. However, Wiseman's infrared video recordings were able to show precisely what had gone on. There was nothing inexplicable or supernatural. As with previous experiments, his 1999 participants' impressions of what had happened at the seances were affected by the atmosphere of the occasion, the darkness, the creepy music and the suggestions planted in their minds by the 'medium'. Wiseman has found that participants who believed in the possibility of contact with the spirit world were significantly more likely to report experiencing things which never happened. Conversely, sceptics were more likely to deny witnessing events which in reality did occur.

Where suggestibility is known to occur, there will always be those willing to exploit it. There will be an interest in those who claim that they can contact the spirit world for as long as there are grieving people looking for reassurance and curious people looking for knowledge. It cannot be said categorically that through clairvoyance, or at seances, nothing extraordinary happens. Neither can it be stated with absolute conviction that if extraordinary things do happen they come from another dimension of existence – perhaps one beyond the grave.

What does appear to be the case, however, is that from information supposedly received from 'the other side', we learn little about the world beyond: our knowledge is not advanced. Messages received through mediumship tend to be trite and banal. Even the music supposedly sent by long-dead composers to modern-day amanuenses is little more than pastiche. I have several times been played tapes by people who believe that they have spoken to the dead and who recorded their words. The words are spoken by these people themselves in distorted voices. At the time of recording, I was told, the intermediary had been in a trance. Strangely the voices are always said to be those of famous people from the past and they all speak English.

In every case I have examined personally the claims that contact has been made with the dead are easy to disbelieve. Sometimes cases are reported which are harder to understand, and on those occasions hoaxes cannot be ruled out. There was, for instance, the curious case of the computer which appeared to operate itself and leave messages from a seventeenth-century man called Lukas. The ghostly writer had the owner of the computer and the IT experts who examined the evidence entirely baffled. However, a historian with knowledge of the language of the era found too many flaws in the messages expressed and too many unaccountable modern idioms to be convinced that the words had come from a former century.

Once of the most compelling reports of contact by the dead with the living is to be found in an incident relating to Carl Jung and the psychologist Professor James Hyslop with whom he had worked. Professor Hyslop was a close friend of William James, the brother of the writer Henry James. They had made a pact that whoever died first would attempt to make contact with the other from beyond the grave. Jung recounted the following in conversation with Laurens Van der Post.[25]

James died first and Professor Hyslop waited for several years for a sign or message from his friend. One day he received a letter from a husband and wife in Ireland, a country he had never visited. They apologized for troubling him, but said that they communicated with the spirits using a planchette, a device which, so it is said, enables spirits to write messages. They had heard from a William James who insisted that they contact him and give him the message, 'Does he remember the red pyjamas?' It took a while for Hyslop to understand the message and then he recalled how, as young men, they had lost their luggage on a tour of Europe and James had had to buy some immediate necessities. Fancy red pyjamas were the only ones available and Hyslop had teased his friend about his 'dubious taste in nightwear'.

Jung told Van der Post that he had never been concerned that messages from 'the other side' tended to be of a trivial nature. If there were life beyond death, he reasoned, it would be in an idiom which we could not possibly possess in the here and now, and as such was utterly incapable of transmission in terms we can understand. What was surprising, in Jung's view, was not the insignificant nature of the messages, but the fact that they were received at all. Reflecting on Jung's comments, Van der Post went one stage further. He argued that the seemingly trivial messages might indeed be full of hidden meaning. In the case of the red pyjamas, that message had been concerned with a journey taken by the two friends to a place neither had visited before. The luggage, which was lost, represented the impedimenta of life. The pyjamas represented sleep, peace and rest.

It is a remarkable story, but notwithstanding the eminence of those involved and retelling it, it should not be forgotten that it came to Van der Post third-hand. Had it by then taken on the characteristics of legend, a story which develops in the telling in order to strengthen, or embellish, the ideas which it is attempting to convey. Who were the couple from Ireland? Were they investigated? Might they have been involved, even if unknowingly, in a hoax designed by someone who knew of the pact between Hyslop and James? Was telepathy involved rather than spirit communication? The story cannot be accepted at face value, although it remains an intriguing one.

There are many reported cases of very specific messages being received by ordinary people from the famous dead. There are several websites claiming to contain messages from Princess Diana confirming that she is carrying on her humanitarian work from the spirit world. There is no way of knowing whether the originators of the websites are pranksters or sincere. A book has been published by an American woman and her partner who describe having regular contact with Elvis Presley. She says that through her psychic communications she has discovered Elvis' true purpose. He came, she says, from another galaxy, to bring enlightenment and wisdom to the world. She tells of her psychic encounters with Elvis in earnest tones and does not appear to be intentionally misleading her readers.

What is frequently revealed in messages from the famous from 'the other side' is nothing which could not have been written by an imaginative fiction writer. No insights are vouchsafed, no hidden knowledge is revealed. That is not to accuse everyone claiming to take down dictation from the 'next world' that they are involved in a fraud, although some will be. It is to suggest that the ideas recorded are derived from this side of any divide and not the other. The stigmatic Heather Woods produced tens of thousands of words of automatic, or 'spirit' writing. Her spirit writing was done with her left hand, while normally she was right-handed. She employed a range of handwriting styles. She said that she was acting on behalf of several famous mystics and prophets of history, including Kahlil Gibran, the author of *The Prophet* – yet my examination of her output revealed nothing original or enlightening. The words were found to be encouraging to those looking for such encouragement, but were not original in either content or form – good pastiche, but not more. This poem on the subject of death is one of the best examples:

> If death should beckon me with outstretched hand,
> And whisper softly of 'an unknown land',
> I shall not be afraid to go,
> For though the path I do not know,
> I take death's hand without a fear,
> For He who safely brought me here,
> Will also take me back.
> And though in many ways I lack,
> He will not let me go alone,
> Into the 'valley that's unknown',
> So I reach out and take death's hand,
> And journey to the Promised Land.

One should not approach the subject with a closed mind. It may indeed be the case that great insights have been shared through the employment of psychic gifts, but those insights have been personal insights. They have not been conveyed to others and widely shared because no adequate language exists to convey them. Thus it is that if contact has been genuinely made by contactees with the world to come – and that is a hypothesis which remains unproven – nothing of the wisdom of the world beyond has as yet been conveyed back to earth using mediumship or psychic powers. Perhaps that wisdom which goes beyond language is given to us in other ways – through music, poetry or the visual arts. It comes maybe in the form of artistic inspiration. If that is the case, it does not identify its source, and to say that it is evidence of communication from the spirit world is again unproven.

Of all the many types of alleged contact between this world and the next, one has been subjected to considerable scientific examination. The data on ghosts appears to suggest that events take place which are unexplained, but which have yielded to measurement. The sounds of alleged ghosts have been recorded as have photographic images. In one case, that of the haunted theatre in Margate in Kent, a ghost was captured briefly by a video camera on two occasions – once in vision and once in sound.[26]

In fiction ghosts are sometimes described as earthbound spirits. In some cases they interact, unseen, with the living. Ghosts associated with particular places are said to be imprints of the spirit left behind. There are several types of ghost or apparition:

Firstly, there are those who appear just once to a specific person. This is said to happen at the point of death when a departing soul takes its leave. Ethel Chapman, the Anglican stigmatic, described how people who were dying would come to her in the night in her room at the Leonard Cheshire Home where she lived on the outskirts of Liverpool. In another example, a man who had nursed his mother through dementia finally allowed himself to have her looked after in a home. In the middle of one night he suddenly felt extremely ill and vomited violently. Ten minutes later he had a telephone call from the home to say that his mother had just died.

Secondly, there are the visions of the dead seen shortly after death as if to comfort the relatives or to complete a task. It could be argued that the appearance of the risen Christ falls into this category. More recently there were the many reports of the ghost of Elvis Presley appearing to his followers.

Thirdly, there are the appearances of scenes or pageants from the past which appear to be imprinted on a place. Witnesses to these have reported hearing the sound of fighting on ancient battlefields. One well-known example concerns a Roman army seen to be marching through the walls under York Minster, taking the route of an old Roman thoroughfare.[27]

Fourthly, there are deathbed visions which appear to those about to die and are interpreted as spirits from the other side come to guide the dying person on a journey. In one instance, a woman who had had Alzheimer's disease for many years and had been totally incapacitated physically and mentally, sat up in bed moments before her death, with a smile on her face and arms open as if in greeting.[28]

A poll conducted in the USA in the 1980s revealed that 42 per cent of the adult population and 67 per cent of widows reported sensing apparitions of the dead. Not all were sightings; some heard voices and others were touched.

Few people deny that ghosts are experienced. There is, however, no agreement as to what they are. Are they a product of a kind of dreamlike state when the imagination is able to conjure up ideas from the subconscious and give them tangible, olfactory, visible or audible life? Is telepathy involved between the living, rather than the dead, with messages about death being transmitted by one living person to another? Can images of the past become locked into the materials of this earth in the way that sound can be preserved on tape or moving pictures on film? There are many fascinating possibilities and they do not all require a belief in the afterlife. They may be products of current time and space to which people have attached a spiritual or futuristic meaning.

The psychiatrist Dr Elisabeth Kübler-Ross, whose study of the experiences of the dying have extended the boundaries of knowledge on the mental processes involved in facing death, also entered the debate about the afterlife. She expressed a belief in reincarnation,[29] a courageous statement of faith for a respected scientist to make if she wished to retain her credibility in medical circles. She also claimed that humans have spirit guides to help them at times of stress – that after death they are reunited with people they have loved who have preceded them, and that, as we approach death, we know when it is about to happen. She also thought that a judgement would occur, but that this would be in the form of a self-analysis of one's life. This idea is not new and can be found in Plato's *The Republic*. In this classic work of philosophical dialogue a story is told of a soldier who appears to rise from the dead after being killed in battle. He comes back with tales of the afterworld and tells of how sinners have to choose how to be reborn according to their own review of their past life.[30] *The Tibetan Book of the Dead* which, it is thought, dates from over 1,000 years ago, also features self-judgement in the next life.

Dr Kübler-Ross went further than speculating about life after death: she told of how she believed she had once had a visit from someone who was dead. She told of how she had met the ghost of a former patient. Apparently Dr Kübler-Ross was on the verge of giving up her work through exhaustion when she saw the apparition. Her dead patient beseeched her not to retire. She continued with her work.

There is one further area of evidence which suggests that life on earth is not the only plane of existence. It might or might not be interpreted as evidence of an afterlife, but it is taken as evidence that worlds lie beyond our immediate senses. This area of study is one familiar to Christians and concerns angels. The Bible is full of angels as messengers. They come to earth from heaven to warn or alert. It is also said that everyone has a guardian angel, a spirit guide, watching and protecting.[31] A belief in a personal angelic minder is commonly found among Christians. In other cultures guardian spirits and spirit guides are described. There are several organizations which hold courses to enable, so they claim, individuals to make contact with their ethereal guardians.

One spectacular instance of angel protection occurred in Kent as recently as 1991. The brakes of a bus failed on a steep hill and the driver lost control. One of the passengers recalls the driver shouting for everyone to get to the back of the bus. 'Then I saw these angels, six or eight of them, out of the window and floating at about half the height of the bus. They were wearing long creamy-whitish gowns like nighties, had blonde hair and the most beautiful faces. They formed a line and put their hands out to stop the bus and gradually, it came to a halt, inches from a brick wall.' A later inspection of the bus confirmed that the brakes had seized up and there was no way it should have been able to stop.[32] When one researcher advertised for personal accounts of angels, 1,500 people responded. Many of the accounts involved people being specifically aware of their guardian angels. There are also said to be archangels and cherubim and seraphim – indeed a hierarchy of these spiritual beings who worship God and do his bidding, except those who have fallen with Satan.[33]

By convention angels are represented in art as winged beings. No detailed or anatomical description of angels is given in the Bible, apart from that in Isaiah 6:2, which describes the wings of the seraphim. Other faiths acknowledge the angelic dimension and some religions talk of a range of demons and spirit beings. In Islam there are jinn or genies, for instance, which are an order of spiritual being lower in the celestial hierarchy than the angels.

The appearance of angels as beings from heaven is not restricted to biblical times. Mystical and unconventional writers from Emmanuel Swedenborg[34] to William Blake[35] to Rudolf Steiner[36] have described their belief in the angelic realms. Swedenborg's visions took him to heaven and hell where he communicated, he said, with the angels. Their thoughts came to him as flashes into his mind. Blake saw angels sitting in the branches of trees and spoke to them. Steiner wrote extensively on angels as spirits of personality living in waves of time, changing their spiritual bodies from age to age.

The modern belief in angels is strong enough for a genre of angel books to be commercially viable, along with such magazines as *Angel Times*, based in America. A relatively modern angelic visitation, or at least a claim of one, has had a major influence on American religious life. It was an angel called Moroni who appeared to Joseph Smith, founder of the Mormons, in 1823 and gave him the text of a new scripture, *The Book of Mormon*. The Mormons, who have their own capital city and base in Utah, are now one of the fastest growing post-Christian churches in the world.

There are many stories told of visits by individual angels to people at times of crisis. The Shackleton Antarctic expedition came back with a strange tale of an extra member who helped them with their work. Even more fantastic, reported Stuart Gordon, was the story smuggled out of Russia concerning the Soyuz 7 space station. The three cosmonauts on board were suddenly amazed to see a brilliant orange light. 'They saw seven giant figures in the form of humans, but with wings and mist-like halos as in the classic depiction of angels. They appeared to be hundreds of feet tall... they followed the space craft for several minutes, vanished and returned twelve days later. "They were smiling as though they shared a glorious secret," one cosmonaut recalled.' [37]

It is interesting that while the cosmonauts, products of the secular Soviet state, chose to describe the curious phenomenon they witnessed as angelic, some in the 'Christian' West have preferred to describe the strange figures as aliens. Indeed there are some people who believe that all reports of angels, even those from the Bible, are in fact reports of visiting aliens from other advanced civilizations.

The best-known example of a recent claim of angelic intervention must be that of the Angels of Mons. In August 1914, during one of the earliest military encounters between the Germans and the allied troops in the First World War, it is said that angels appeared on the battlefield to reduce the carnage. One man saw an angel with outstretched wings. Another spoke of a strange light and three shapes, one of which had wings. German sources confirmed the strange sightings, which caused horses to turn and flee.

If sightings of angels are not sightings of messengers from heaven, what are they? Could they be expressions of our own deep psyche tapping into the collective memory from which all archetypes are drawn? We cannot tell, yet angels have been very real to many and continue to play an essential role in the living mythology of our time and culture. Very recently, the massive sculpture of the angel of the north erected near Newcastle upon Tyne has attracted huge interest and debate in Britain.

Angels are said to have a specific role to play when a person dies. Swedenborg believed that there existed a special group of angelic beings who helped people make the transition from the bodily life to the spiritual life. In his book on the visionary's work Robert Kirven described how Swedenborg believed that when a dying person says something strange or incomprehensible to onlookers, it could be that the person is addressing the angels. Angels come like ethereal medical attendants to offer their care. Those who are particularly unprepared for their transition to a completely spiritual life, either because they die suddenly or do not expect to live after death, need special help. Swedenborg described how people wake up gradually after death and become aware of angels whose radiant love they find especially comforting. After new arrivals in the afterlife accept their changed situation, he taught, and many do with little help, they begin to meet angelic spirits more like themselves. If they are confused they will be counselled by angel teachers. In Swedenborg's vision of life after death, angels of all kinds exist to help. There is much for a human to learn about being a spirit, he said.[38]

Swedenborg's is a very specific and idiosyncratic vision of the afterlife. Two centuries after he lived he still has a dedicated band of followers who value his teaching as a great and comforting insight into the mysteries of the human existence. Who knows whether he was a man who had truly valuable insights to offer or whether he was just a highly imaginative writer and narrator of fanciful ideas?

Angels are an essential part of Christmas. They are to be found playing a key role in the story. They came to the shepherds as the heralds of the good news of the birth of Jesus. They also come to warn and to announce.[39] Christmas carols such as 'Angels from the Realms of Glory' are full of angels. School nativity plays often include dozens of angels on stage, dressed in white with tinsel halos; it is a very good way of making sure every child has a part. The angels of the Christmas story in the gospels capture the imagination, perhaps bring the faithful nearer to God, even though we have no way of knowing exactly what or who they are.

In some ways the same can be said of so many of the supernatural phenomena which are thought to provide proof of the hereafter. Logically one can dismiss reincarnation, clairvoyance or near-death experiences as delusions or hallucinations, but strangely, in many cases, those who have direct experience of such events and phenomena find themselves moved by them in some spiritual way. The experience can enhance faith or lead to faith. Exactly what kind of faith, of course, is another matter.

There are precedents for almost all these phenomena to be found in the Christian scriptures. That a phenomenon is mentioned does not, of course, imply approval. Nor does it prove that a phenomenon has an independent exterior existence. Arguably ghosts and angels could all be products of the inner self. To discern Christian teaching on evidence of the afterlife requires examining the many, apparently confusing items of evidence in relation to each other, and in the context of Christian tradition.

CHAPTER FIVE

Scripture and Tradition

There is one area of Christian practice that involves contact by those living with those who are dead. It is that of intercessionary prayer. Especially in the Roman Catholic tradition, Christians direct their prayers to God through a saint, or holy figure, with whom they feel an empathy and to whom they show a special devotion. Most commonly it is Mary, mother of Jesus, who is the object of this piety. The rosary, the most popular form of Catholic meditative prayer, is directed in this way: 'Holy Mary, Mother of God, pray for us sinners, now and at the hour of our death.'

There are saints in the calendar identified with particular professions or needs to whom prayers may be directed, and if all else fails there is St Jude, patron saint of lost causes. For someone to be recognized as a saint, the Roman Catholic Church requires evidence of a miracle attributed to the intervention of this holy person from beyond the grave. Claims of miracles are systematically and thoroughly examined. Vatican officials – and there is a whole department in Rome dealing with claims, or causes as they are known – require detailed evidence. In the case of a healing miracle they need medical documentation confirming a patient's condition before an alleged cure and medical evidence confirming the change which has taken place. In addition medical science must provide evidence that the recovery by the patient cannot be explained by natural means or attributed to medical treatment. A wide-ranging and minute inquiry into the candidate's life is also undertaken. This is the modern process, formalized in the seventeenth century, although before this a tradition of local veneration was often sufficient for an individual's sanctity to be recognized. The Orthodox churches have their own less rigorous and formalized system while the Protestant traditions do not practise canonization.

The present pope is believed to have approved the canonization of more saints than any of his predecessors. This does not mean he has created more saints – that is not within his power. However he has acknowledged more people than ever before to be saints in heaven. Once the claim made on behalf of a potential saint's followers has been accepted, this amounts to the official recognition that intervention has occurred by someone of the other world in this. However, it does not follow that the saint themselves has intervened, only that God has intervened at the request of the saint. The communication with the dead soul is thus one-way and not two-way.

The exception to this might be said to apply to Mary, mother of Jesus. She has a special status in Catholic tradition and is said to appear and intervene in this world directly. She is no ordinary saint and an outside observer viewing an especially pious Marian group might suppose she is afforded the status of demi-God rather than saint. Standard Roman Catholic teaching, as it pertains to Mary, is contained in *Faith Alive*, the 1988 officially sanctioned presentation of Catholic faith.[1]

The first two stanzas of the rosary prayer are quotations, *Faith Alive* explains, from Luke's Gospel. 'Hail Mary, full of Grace, the Lord is with thee,' are the words of the annunciation by the Archangel Gabriel when Mary is told that she is to be the mother of Jesus.[2] The words, 'Blessed art thou among women, and blessed is the fruit of thy womb,' are those of Mary's cousin Elizabeth, mother of John the Baptist.[3] The third part, 'Holy Mary, Mother of God, pray for us sinners, now and at the hour of our death,' was added to the biblical quotes by the 'devotional tradition of the Church'.

> By this, we turn a Scripture meditation on the Annunciation and the Visitation into a prayer, a personal address to our spiritual mother. Just as we ask other Christians on this earth to pray for us, so now we join the 'communion of saints' in heaven by faith, asking the 'Queen of Saints and Angels' to pray for us. Note that the prayer is going back eventually to God. It does not stop at Mary. She prays for us to God.[4]

Mary is invoked on many occasions and she is given titles to associate her with specific pleadings or concerns. Our Lady of Sorrows and Our Lady of the Poor are two examples of the genre. A belief in the intercession of the saints does not, however, amount to a proof in the afterlife, nor does it add to our knowledge of an existence beyond death. If it is true that prayers directed to God through a saint are answered – and again this is matter which can only be accepted in faith and cannot be proven – then that indicates that while God answers prayers there is not necessarily any role played by the saint in him doing so. It would indicate that God can intervene in the world, but it is not giving us any further enlightenment as to what the realms beyond death are like.

If God can intervene, it does not appear in Christian teaching that there is any encouragement for the dead to contact the living. In the story of the rich man in hell and the poor man Lazarus in the arms of Abraham, as told by Luke, the rich man asks if Lazarus could be sent from the other side of the grave to warn his brothers to change their ways and 'not come to this place of torment': 'But Abraham said, "They have Moses and the prophets; let them listen to them." "No, father Abraham," [the rich man] replied, "but if someone from the dead visits them, they will repent." Abraham answered, "If they do not listen to Moses and the prophets they will pay no heed even if someone should rise from the dead.""[5] As with so many of the gospel parables, the story has a two-edged message. It is not simply about ghosts returning to warn the living; it also looks ahead to the day when there will be many in the world who will reject the gospel of the risen Christ.

God's revelation of purpose and knowledge is to be found, so Christians believe, in the scriptures. Searching the Bible for clues as to what lies beyond death, however, is a confusing quest. An examination of some of the books of the Old Testament, Ecclesiastes or Job, for instance, can lead to the conclusion that nothing is beyond. The words of Christ suggest something is beyond, but exactly what is only hinted at enigmatically. The penitent thief at the crucifixion is told that he will be with Christ that day, after death, in paradise.[6] But how can this be? Do Christians not declare in the Nicean Creed that Christ descended into hell before rising again? Should reading the Bible too literally carry some form of spiritual health warning? Sorting the allegory from the poetry from the history from the prophecy, all of which are to be found on the pages of the Bible, is the most daunting of tasks.

However a search through the texts for some of the main references to death and its meaning can be undertaken. The first death reported in the Bible is a murder. It is to be found in Genesis in the story of the murder of Abel by his brother Cain.[7] No hint is given as to what becomes of Abel in an afterlife, but through his deed Cain discovers the existence of death and, through his punishment for murder, he learns to fear the consequences of killing. The story states emphatically that it is not permissible for a person to kill a fellow human being created in the image of God. Later, in the ten commandments, that direction from God is confirmed formally.[8] The exception, however, allowed to the Israelites was that killing as a punishment was permitted, and not just for murder. Stoning to death as a punishment for adultery was prescribed, as it was for persistently and deliberately erroneous teachers. No indication is given as to what the offender might expect to experience after death. Having the one God, the Israelites did not share in the wider religious practices of their Middle Eastern neighbours of worshipping a specific God of the dead. For instance, the Canaanites of the second millennium BC, best known as the worshippers of Baal, recognized a god of death, named Mot. A god of death, in any religion which has one, is seen as the god who controls the afterlife and determines the destiny of those who die. Without a god of death the Jews appeared to have little concept of the destiny awaiting the dead.

The Jewish law contained detailed instructions as to what should happen at the time of a death. In Deuteronomy, for instance, the brother of a man who dies childless is instructed to marry the widow in order to father a son.[9] Instructions of this kind, combined with the belief that the sins of the fathers can be visited on the children, treat death not so much as the end of an individual's life on earth, but an event of importance to the family or tribe. As in several cultures today, identity is derived not so much from an individual's distinctiveness, but from his or her position within a wider social setting.

Separating the individual from the group is a relatively modern concept. It is a defining element of modern Western liberalism from which such notions as individual rights have evolved. To most cultures, past and present, individuality would have been an alien concept, and even within the modern Western tradition the idea is challenged. When Jung refers to humans having a collective unconscious,[10] Rupert Sheldrake writes of morphic resonance[11] and Ian Marshall expounds his beehive theory,[12] they all anchor the individual's being in a collective rather than an individual purpose.

Sheldrake suggests that knowledge acquired by an individual member of any species, *Homo sapiens* included, is somehow transmitted to everyone within the group as shared knowledge, without there needing to be direct contact or communication. An example of morphic resonance, as he called this transmission of information, was observed in the case of the blue tit. When the first blue tit discovered how to open a bottle of milk on a doorstep, blue tits hundreds of miles away acquired the same skill almost simultaneously.[13]

Marshall's beehive theory suggests that the dissemination of culturally shared ideas permeates from our waking into our unconscious states,[14] in a way not dissimilar to Jung's collective unconscious whereby, in our conscious state, we all draw on shared images, fears and archetypes held somehow communally, but unknowingly, by all human beings.[15]

Such thinking is relevant to our search for clues as to what happens after death. Buddhists and others suggest that the ultimate purpose is to reach a state where the individual – the ego – is subsumed into something greater.

As the history of the Jewish people unfolds in the Old Testament, evidence is presented which suggests that it was believed that the spirit of an individual who had died survived the death of the body and could be contacted. After the death of the prophet Samuel, Saul consulted a medium, the witch of Endor. He went to her in disguise, as he had himself outlawed mediumship and did not wish to be recognized. However she saw through his disguise. Saul swore that she would not be punished for practising her art and she summoned up the spirit of Samuel. 'Why hast thou disquieted me, to bring me up?' demanded the prophet. And as if to demonstrate that summoning up the dead was a dangerous and risky practice, Saul was given the news that he did not wish to hear, that the Philistines would defeat the Israelites and that he would die. The words of the dead Samuel, as reported by the witch of Endor, imply a belief that the dead are in a state of sleep.[16] At the death of King David the Bible uses the words, 'So David rested with his forefathers and was buried in the city of David.'[17]

Did the dead later awake? The Old Testament gives few clues, and those it does give are tantalizing rather than definitive. In the book of Daniel the Jews are given a vision of the end-time when the Archangel Michael will appear. The end-time is a term used in several religions to describe that moment when life on earth will cease and God will judge all humankind: 'And many of them that sleep in the dust of the earth shall awake, some to everlasting life, and some to shame and everlasting contempt. And they that be wise shall shine as the brightness of the firmament; and they that turn many to righteousness as the stars for ever and ever.'[18] Isaiah gives a similar promise of what is to come: 'dead men shall live… Awake and sing, ye that dwell in dust: for thy dew is as the dew of herbs, and the earth shall cast out the dead.'[19] It is all, however, set at some time in an undefined future. From this it seems the dead are not sent to another world, but rest in the grave to wait the final fulfilment of God's purpose.

Modern Jews, divided as they are into a spectrum of traditions from ultra-orthodox to very liberal, not surprisingly, take a range of views. 'If you ask me what I believe will happen when I die,' says the liberal Rabbi Julia Neuberger,

> I have to say personally I think it is probably nothing… One cannot tell and it seems to me that speculation is pointless. One must live as if this life is the only one we have and should there be another, then that will be a bonus. Most Jews, particularly orthodox Jews, would not be so adamant. But Judaism does stress 'this life' beyond any other possibilities, and we know that in this life we can affect what happens to ourselves and others.[20]

Another liberal rabbi, Dr Sidney Brichto, writes of his belief in immortality, but says that the essence of the divine promise of immortality is the affirmation of the ultimate value of each human life:

> The Rabbis of old said that he who saves a single life saves the world and he who destroys a life destroys the world. The belief in the immortal life of the human soul should not be a sop to those who suffer in this life by the promise of something better in the World to Come. It is far better to live as though it were all happening here and now. We should seek our immortality in the effect we have on others by what we do and what we say.[21]

Not that Rabbi Sidney Brichto would have had the support of the Jewish, but irreligious, Woody Allen, who once observed that he did not wish to achieve immortality through his work: 'I want to achieve it through not dying.'[22]

The ancient Jewish approach differed greatly from that of many of the other cultures at the time of the Jewish kings. The Israelites had one God, whereas the contemporary pantheistic religions had different gods, each with different responsibilities. As mentioned above in relation to the Canaanites, a god of death, or lord of the underworld, was frequently described. The Sumerian religious system taught that a king and queen by the names of Nergal and Eresh-Kigal ruled the underworld as their independent dominion. The Mithras cult of the Romans taught followers that death was a terrifying initiation through which the soul passed in order to find light and purity. The Egyptians believed that Osiris, who in life had been both man and god, had been resurrected from the dead to rule over the world of the dead.

The legend of Osiris is a disturbing one for Christians. It tells a story of death and resurrection which bears some similarity to that of the Christian faith. In the legend the dismembered body of Osiris is pieced together and restored to life, and thereafter he reigns as king over the dead in the other world, bearing the titles Lord of the Underworld and Lord of Eternity. He presides in judgement over the souls of the departed who receive the appropriate reward for their virtue – eternal life – or punishment for their sins. 'In the resurrection of Osiris, the Egyptians saw the pledge of a life everlasting for themselves beyond the grave,' wrote Sir James Frazer in *The Golden Bough*.[23]

However the promise of eternal life could only be fulfilled if the surviving friends and relatives of the deceased observed the correct funeral rites. In this regard the Osiris myth and the Christian story differ radically in their teaching, although it should be pointed out that echoes of the Egyptian belief survive in some Christian practices and that the Jewish people of Jesus' day set great store by the proper observation of burial rites. For good reasons of public hygiene, Jewish law stipulated that burial of a body should not be delayed and the culture of the day ensured that burial was conducted piously and reverently. In many Christian countries, performing funeral rituals in the correct manner is considered to be very important. Graves, it is said, should only be dug in consecrated ground. That ground should then remain hallowed. The correct formulae of words, the last rites, should be said, preferably by a priest, as close to the moment of death as possible.

One of the most important prayers of the Roman Catholic Church in this context is that which symbolically releases the soul:

> Go forth, Christian soul, from this world,
> in the name of God the almighty father who created you,
> in the name of Jesus Christ, Son of the living God, who suffered
>   for you,
> In the name of the Holy Spirit, who was poured out upon you.
> Go forth, faithful Christian.
> May you live in peace this day,
> may your home be with God in Zion,
> with Mary, the virgin mother of God,
> with Joseph, and all the angels and saints.[24]

In Catholic tradition many believe that prayers for the departed can help them through the trials of purgatory. Purgatory is the state through which the dead are said to pass to be cleansed before entering the presence of God. A tradition grew up within Catholicism whereby the living prayed for the dead to speed up their time in purgatory and so hasten them on their way to the divine presence. In medieval times the tradition was notoriously abused when the Church sold indulgences and before death the rich paid large sums of money to the Church in exchange for an early release from the state of purgatory.

Also, around a century before the Christian era, it was recorded in the first book of Maccabees, one of the important Jewish texts not included in the main canon of the Old Testament, that Jews prayed for those who had fallen in battle, especially if they had died in disobedience to Jewish law and had been wearing idolatrous charms when they were killed.

The story of Osiris is less troublesome to a Christian if it is seen as an archetypal story. It presents a set of ideas which occur in several cultures. It does not seem unreasonable to suppose that if God creates archetypes he should then employ archetypes to convey his truth.

Despite being full of accounts of death in all its forms, ranging from natural death to murder, or genocide – indeed in the story of Noah the death of almost every member of the human race – the Old Testament gives surprisingly few hints as to what follows death. As Professor John Bowker writes in his Bible commentary, 'This is one of the most extraordinary facts of the Bible. Virtually the whole of the Hebrew Bible came into being without any belief that faith would be rewarded after death.'[25]

He finds few biblical texts, in addition to those already quoted above, that give any clear indication of a belief in life after death. Two are to be found in the Psalms and are among the very few indications that righteousness on this earth or suffering in this world will be rewarded in the next. Psalm 49 says for those who prosper here on earth that death is the end: '[Man] is like the beasts that perish... Like sheep they are laid in the grave; death shall feed on them.' To which the psalmist adds, 'God will redeem my soul from the power of the grave: for he shall receive me,' as compensation for his innocent suffering in exile.[26] And Psalm 73 contains these two verses: 'Thou shalt guide me with thy counsel, and afterward receive me to glory. Whom have I in heaven but thee?'[27]

In the Old Testament book of Ecclesiastes there is an intriguing passage which not only implies that death is the end, but also that the end is superior to the beginning. The book is attributed to King Solomon, who in legend is noted for his great wisdom:

A good name smells sweeter than the finest ointment, and the day of death is better than the day of birth. Better to visit the house of mourning than the house of feasting; for to be mourned is the lot of every man, and the living should take this to heart. Grief is better than laughter: a sad face may go with a cheerful heart. Wise men's thoughts are at home in the house of mourning, but a fool's thoughts in the house of mirth... Better the end of anything than its beginnings.[28]

There are also passages to be found in the books of the prophets that suggest a belief in resurrection, notably Hosea, Isaiah and Ezekiel, but Bowker suggests that in their context they are more probably 'graphic metaphors describing the future restoration of the whole people'. In other words they may be passages describing how Israel as a nation will be resurrected and are not to be taken as descriptions of the bodily resurrection of the dead. The best-known example of a passage of this kind can be found in Ezekiel 37 where the prophet describes his vision of the restoration of the dry bones:

The hand of the Lord was upon me... and set me down in the midst of the valley which was full of bones... And he said unto me, Son of man, can these bones live? And I answered, O Lord God, thou knowest. Again he said unto me, Prophesy upon these bones, and say unto them, O ye dry bones, hear the word of the Lord. Thus saith the Lord God unto these bones; Behold, I will cause breath to enter into you, and ye shall live.[29]

In addition there is some suggestion that exceptional individuals, such as Elijah, Abraham and Moses, were allowed into heaven without needing to rest in the grave until the day of judgement. Generally, however, the idea of life after death is sketchy and marginal.

By the time of Jesus the notion of the resurrection of the dead had grown in importance as a matter of Jewish faith. It was a time of great expectation. Not only was a messiah expected, but so were cosmic disturbances which would end the known world order. There would be a judgement of nations and the resurrection of the ancestors. The Anglican position on this subject has been formally expressed in this way. Reviewing the evidence of the Old Testament it notes that the state of the dead is one of non-existence:

> By New Testament times however, most Jews had come to believe in a future state in which the injustices of the earthly life are done away with. Between the individual's death and the general resurrection the soul, separated from the body, would go to a place of waiting, where the reversal of destiny for the successful oppressor and the undeserving sufferer could already begin. God was seen as the judge who weighs the life of the individual... Thus Judaism affirms that God's sovereignty extends to the dead as well as the living, so that the righteous of every generation are destined to have their share in the everlasting kingdom.[30]

To the Jewish people of earlier times, the era of the Hebrew Bible, human beings were created by God from ordinary material and matter and he had then breathed life into them. Blood was the key to life, not an immaterial soul. Thus once the blood ceased to flow, or blood was shed, and the body was dead, there was nothing to go on to another world, paradise or plane of existence. As the body lay in the grave the dead survived in shadow form as memory, dream and through descendants.

This view of life after death was, as Professor Bowker writes, 'scarcely vigorous, and that is why the Hebrew Bible is mostly concerned with avoiding or postponing death, relying instead on the power of God to deliver the living from falling into the pit, or grave'.[31]

What exactly happened to the exceptionally righteous, who were exempt from the grave, the Jewish tradition does not explain. One idea about which there was speculation was that survival beyond death took the form of a resurrection of the body. There was also the idea, echoed in

Greek tradition, that the soul might be gifted immortality. 'No one knew,' wrote John Bowker. 'The Bible does not say, and early Christians simply put the two ideas together. More important is the trust in God that the One who creates in the first place will continue to do so in the future.'[32]

Christians are sometimes accused of being obsessed with death. They pray about it, talk about it, sing about it every Sunday. Some believers even wear a chain around their neck to which is attached a small replica of a dying man being gruesomely executed – though that is not the way the wearer perceives of the crucifix. The crucifix, to the Christian, is a symbol of loving sacrifice, not death by execution. Yet certainly Christians celebrate the death of Jesus Christ, their religion's founder who is also believed to be the Son of God and their saviour. In some traditions of Christianity the faithful glory in every gory detail of his prolonged and agonizing end. Since the thirteenth century, when the passion of Christ became the focus of much devotion in the Roman Catholic world, religious artists have not held back from depicting the crucifixion of Christ in the greatest blood-red detail.

Christians claim that through the death of Jesus in all its horror, and then through his subsequent resurrection in all its magnificence, Jesus has released them from the power of death itself. He conquered death and sin, they proclaim – almost as if the two were the same thing, which in one sense they are, if death in this context means spiritual death. But in another sense, physical death is far from sinful. It is inevitable. While it can often be a distressing affair, death can also be peaceful – almost a joyful conclusion to life.

Death, in the physical sense, comes in many guises. No two deaths are identical, although death can be divided into two main categories – natural and traumatic. When it comes to spiritual death there are no neat categories. And spiritual life and spiritual death lie at the heart of the Christian message. Often this message is presented negatively: it is sin and death which are emphasized. Many churches play on guilt, leaving the glories of spiritual life unheralded. The spiritual stick is used to beat the sinners; the spiritual carrot is kept well out of sight. There are some horrendous stories told of how children can be terrified by overzealous teachers, pastors, priests and even parents in the course of their religious upbringing. Many who went through the Roman Catholic educational system lost their faith as a result, but never lost their sense of guilt. Equally there are the offspring of Protestants whose lives as children were overshadowed by a pall of guilt. Everything they did was deemed sinful and sin had fatal consequences. Many children have been damaged by an overzealous religious upbringing. They have found it difficult to form adult relationships, especially with those of the opposite sex. Many have rejected the good as well as the bad in their childhood and have become estranged from their parents. 'What are the wages of sin?' they were asked as children and they had to respond that it was death.

There many Christian traditions which have appeared to concentrate on the wickedness of the individual, often to the exclusion of rejoicing in the glory of God. It is as if these traditional strands of faith protest too much and are almost glorying vicariously in the sin as they condemn it. They talk about being released from the power of death by the blood of Jesus, but is it just talk? Are they hiding from their fear of death – and not just spiritual death, but physical death as well? And how fair and true are these traditions in interpreting the Christian view of death?

Perhaps the concentration on the fear, rather than the hope, of what is to come after death can be accounted for in a different way. The Church is, in one sense, embarrassed by its ignorance. It preaches loudly against sin and the wages of eternal damnation. It can conjure up horrendous images of hell and torture. It preaches a gospel of eternal life and talks of rewards in heaven and yet it cannot offer any image of the glory to come. There are many Christians who find it easy to frighten themselves, and others, by imagining hell and yet they find it almost impossible to imagine heaven.

As a result the issue is dodged. A very good example of this is to be found in the Archbishop of Canterbury's *Millennium Message*, published as a short, easy-to-read paperback to put the Christian message back into the millennium celebrations. Many people discover faith at a time of crisis in their lives. They find themselves facing the fundamental mysteries of existence and look for answers. One of the most common times when this happens is at the time of the death of someone very close.

An introductory booklet about Christianity one might have supposed would have addressed the issues surrounding death. Dr Carey talks about Jesus offering an eternal solution to the guilt and shame of our many mistakes and spends a long time describing the theology of the crucifixion and resurrection in a way that would interest a committed Christian rather than a searching agnostic. A great deal of the limited space is spent apologizing for the mistakes the Church has made in the past. There is even a prominent subheading, 'Death: the final and greatest mystery', which occurs on page twenty-nine of fifty-five. We have looked at the facts about Jesus, Dr Carey writes, which we might say have little to do with us directly. They need not affect us at all: 'However, the most important fact of all about Jesus converges with the most important fact of all about each one of us: death. For each of us, the fact of death will end our lives, and we shape our lives according to that fact. But the fact of death did not finish Jesus' life, and that, surely, must interest all of us.'[33]

That is all. Dr Carey continues to discuss a problem of biblical interpretation. As there are four accounts of the death of Jesus in the Bible; can they all be a true record? A subject of interest to scholars and some doubters, but hardly a central issue to address in a unique opportunity to tune into the spiritual needs of the nation at the turn of the millennium.

Twelve years ago several church leaders and writers on religious matters were unable to avoid the question when they were asked to give a clear view on their image of the afterlife for a book being compiled to raise money for the Save the Children Fund. A range of views was expressed. The Free Presbyterian, Ulster politician and Unionist, Revd Dr Ian Paisley, said that the only reliable source on the matter is the Bible: 'The Bible tells us that after death there is judgement. The result of that judgement will be separation – the separation of those who received Christ as Saviour from those who rejected Him. The saved ones shall be with Christ in a heaven of triumph forever. The lost ones shall be without Christ in a hell of torment forever. Relationship to Christ settles our eternal destiny.'[34] His is a clear, black-and-white view which includes a glimpse of the nature of the afterlife as well as the destiny. Heaven is a place of triumph.

A not dissimilar view was expressed by a Roman Catholic priest, Father Andrew Byrne of Opus Dei, the Roman Catholic organization, who in every respect, one would have thought, would have been the very antithesis of Revd Dr Paisley. Indeed many extreme Protestants would barely recognize Father Byrne and his organization as Christian. Yet, like Ian Paisley, Father Byrne firmly stated his belief in hell. He expressed the view that it would be most foolish to forget that only those who love God will be saved. Heaven, presumably in all its glory and triumph, Father Byrne said, was beyond human imagination.[35] As the Apostle Paul wrote, 'Neither eye has seen, nor ear has heard, nor human heart conceived, the welcome God has prepared for those who love him.'[36]

Where Father Byrne and traditional Roman Catholic doctrine part company with Protestant teaching is in the belief in purgatory. Father Byrne calls it a hell with a purpose, a place where sinners will be purged – a painful, but vital process – before they are allowed to see God.

Father Graham Leonard, then Bishop of London, now a Roman Catholic priest having left the Church of England, said he believed that when he died he would be taken into the love of God in a new and deeper way: 'I shall be cleansed and renewed. What is not of God in me will be purged away and what is of God in me will be brought to fulfilment in company with all redeemed in Christ.'[37] He appeared less judgemental than either Father Byrne or Revd Dr Paisley in implying that a process of purging would lie ahead for almost everyone.

'I will go home to God,' when I die, wrote Mother Teresa of Calcutta, 'and will be judged on my love for Him in the poor.'[38] The evangelist Billy Graham wrote in very similar terms. 'When I die the Scriptures teach I will be at home with God forever, along with the many loved ones from all over the world who have trusted Christ and preceded me.'[39] Clearly there is no simple Protestant and Catholic delineation when it comes to images of the afterlife.

What happens after death? That is the wrong question wrote Bruce Kent, the peace campaigner and former Roman Catholic priest:

Not what, Who. God is Father, Brother, companion and friend. He is in mountains, winds and roaring waves but he is also in children's eyes, rabbits and old people walking hand in hand. He is the drive for justice, compassion, generosity and equality… No experience of journeys in this life can compare to the passage from the world we know now to the world which, as St Paul says, we now only see as through a glass, darkly. If, as I believe, the wonders of this world and its beauties are only reflections of the glories of God then I am ready to go in confidence. But how much of 'me' will still be 'me', how that 'me' will relate to the thousands of millions of others, how time that is all at once compares to the time of minutes and hours, all these are mysteries to me.[40]

Malcolm Muggeridge, the rakish journalist, who in the latter years of his life began a search for faith, said that as he grew old the prospect of dying no longer appalled him: 'I await my end hoping it will bring me to a closer walk with God.'[41] Robert Runcie, the former archbishop of Canterbury, once told me that the older he became, the more and more he believed in less and less. In his vision of the afterlife, contributed to the book, he allowed himself no mental picture of life after death, only the profound belief that he felt secure, 'because in death we shall still be in the care of the One we've learnt to trust and who doesn't let us down'.[42]

'The prospect of an existence beyond time and space is incomprehensible,' wrote the great Methodist preacher Dr Donald Soper,

I haven't the mental equipment with which to deal with it. Yet I am not comfortless in as much as Jesus makes no attempt to provide the specific information. He neither included it in his teaching ministry nor offered it to his disciples when he came back to them from the other side of death. Yet he did say that in his Father's house there were many mansions, that he was going on ahead to prepare them for his followers, and that that should be sufficient comfort and assurance of an infinitely worthwhile future beyond the grave. That Gospel will do for me.[43]

Dr John Polkinghorne, the mathematician and priest, like Bruce Kent also quoted Paul's words that we now only see through a glass darkly. What will life be like after death? 'Well, we shall have to wait and see.'[44]

That answer is quite satisfactory to those who are content to trust God. It is an unsatisfactory answer, however, for those who are lacking in trust or who are curious and impatient. Answers to Christian questions can always be found in the New Testament, so it is said by those who embrace a Bible-based religion. So what does the New Testament have to say specifically about life after death?

CHAPTER SIX

The Good News

If it can be said that the Old Testament avoids the issue of what happens after death, then the New Testament is that part of the Bible which deals substantially with the issue, for it relates how, through the death of Jesus, death itself was conquered. Yet does the New Testament give a clear picture of what should be understood by the promise of eternal life?

The Jewish writers of the New Testament remained under the influence of the old. Furthermore they made no attempt to escape from the legacy of the Hebrew scriptures. Time after time, events surrounding the life of Jesus were linked to the words of the Old Testament prophets. Christ's ministry was seen as the fulfilment of the Old Testament. Similarly, the subsequent Gentile interpreters of the New Testament texts have not been able to detach themselves from their Greek, Roman or pagan roots. Thus Christ's words concerning the afterlife have been blended with images from other cultures to produce the words and rituals with which we are familiar today.

Given all these influences, determining what Christian teaching on the afterlife actually is has become a confusing business. Christians believe, in faith, that physical death is not the end. They go further and say that death is a new beginning. But exactly what the individual person who dies experiences and feels after death is never spelled out. A void is left to be filled by the imagination. Additionally, to many outsiders it appears that the Christian attitude to death contains certain internal contradictions. Some non-Christians might wonder why Christians think it is so wrong to kill an unborn foetus, when presumably they believe the child has not sinned, so is destined to go straight to heaven. As a result Christians can be accused of giving a confusing moral lead on many ethical issues – including abortion, capital punishment, war and euthanasia.

These apparent internal contradictions are not always appreciated by those absorbed in their own world of faith. Frequently, as the quotations at the conclusion of the last chapter suggested, church leaders and Christian writers have a view of the afterlife which is tied up with their own religious identity and vested interests here and now. The discrepancies between their views on heaven and hell are exaggerated by the disagreements they have over other aspects of faith and dogma. However, the similarities between Revd Dr Paisley and Father Byrne when it comes to their ideas of judgement and reward are more noteworthy than the differences, even though the two would probably prefer not to have them pointed out.

So what is the unquestionable common ground shared by Christians from all the main traditions? Firstly, it needs to be stated that Christians most certainly believe in eternal life. They believe that through the sacrifice of Christ on the cross of Calvary, death was defeated. They declare in the creeds that there will be a resurrection of the body and that there will be life ever after.

From those beliefs it might be supposed that Christians would not be too concerned about death, seeing earthly life as but a transitory preparation for eternal life. Certainly this was the view taken by many martyrs who faced death for their faith. Throughout history, most Christians have accepted the need to take life. Christian pacifism is only a minority within the churches. The majority of Christians have accepted the need, *in extremis*, of going to war. A just-war theory has evolved to establish the criteria. Also many Christians, by quoting the Old Testament, have been strong advocates of the death penalty. While in more recent times Christians have led campaigns against capital punishment and militarism, for most of the 2,000 years of Christian history, human life has been seen as an expendable commodity. However, Christianity has not gone as far as some religions, such as Islamic Jihad, which have appeared to encourage warfare by promising to soldiers that if killed in battle they will be guaranteed a place in paradise.

Yet, in other contexts, Christians are among the most unyielding defenders of the sanctity of earthly life. It is wrong, they say, to take life. Even lovingly assisting a friend in pain and distress to achieve a hastened end is sinful. Many Christians also vigorously defend life in its embryonic state and equate abortion with infanticide. Christians also need to explain to the confused onlooker why, if there is the promise of eternal life to come, they nevertheless grieve for those who die.

So what do Christians really believe about the afterlife? Is there a place called heaven, a garden of paradise to be enjoyed for ever? There is no single teaching and different traditions and denominations have their own understanding of the issues involved, and their own idiosyncratic ways of expressing their ideas. The biblical sources on the subject are open to several interpretations.

The climax of the New Testament narrative is to be found in the twin events of the crucifixion and the resurrection, and the implications of the two events for humankind. In the creeds, Christians declare that Jesus descended into hell before rising again on the third day.[1] Yet, as mentioned earlier, on the cross Jesus tells the thief crucified with him that that day he will be with him in paradise. Did Jesus go to heaven or hell when he died? While it might be, in the context of his redeeming death, a demeaning and pointless question to ask, there will be many people seeking faith who will want the question answered. There is certainly no clear picture given of either heaven or hell which assists the confused onlooker in understanding better what happened to Jesus immediately after his crucifixion.

The story of the suffering and crucifixion of Jesus is one of, if not the, most moving and powerful ever told. The Son of God is stripped, beaten, humiliated and willingly suffers the agonizing death of a criminal. His corpse is placed hurriedly in a tomb. Three days later the corpse has vanished and a risen Jesus appears to his disciples. Through that one sacrifice of his only son, God is said to have conquered death for all time.

Jesus promised eternal life to those who believed in him. The gospels and the later books of the New Testament are full of hope. Yet where are the clues as to what existence will be like when earthly death comes and the hope of eternal life is fulfilled?

Death, in the New Testament sense, is not simply the cessation of human bodily function. Spiritual death and physical death are not equated. Jesus, so the story of the raising of Lazarus from the dead tells, had the power to raise the physically dead. He could reverse the process of decay. Lazarus was raised when his body was already smelling from putrifaction. Jesus endorsed grief as a natural human response to being physically separated from those we love. He himself wept over Lazarus' tomb before going on to demonstrate that physical death was little different from sleep. He commanded Lazarus to come forth from the tomb.[2] Spiritual death could only be reversed by the individual willingly and knowingly seeking God's grace and mercy. When the rich man asked Jesus what he should do to inherit eternal life, he was told to sell his possessions and give the proceeds to the poor. This he could not bring himself to do.[3]

In the accounts of the resurrection of Jesus himself, no claim is made that the physical body which had been crucified was the one later seen by the disciples. Although the hands, feet and side of the risen Christ's body carried the marks of crucifixion, the body had certain insubstantial qualities. It could pass though doors, vanish from view and, until Jesus was willing to be recognized, remain unrecognizable, even to those who had known Jesus closely during the years of his ministry.

The words of Jesus imply that spiritual death can be experienced while the physical body is still alive. Followers of Christ are told that they must be born again, start life anew. He talks of the kingdom of God to come, but also implies that it is a kingdom which has already arrived. Spiritual death is caused by sin and sinfulness is that state of being when a person is separated from the love of God. Thus a person can be spiritually dead during their earthly life.

Paul elaborated on this teaching in his letter to the Romans:

> you are slaves of the master whom you obey; and this is true whether you serve sin, with death as its result; or obedience with righteousness as its result... But now, freed from the commands of sin, and bound to the service of God, your gains are such as make for holiness, and the end is eternal life. For sin pays a wage, and the wage is death, but God gives freely, and his gift is eternal life, in union with Christ Jesus our Lord.[4]

Spiritual life is eternal and is that which is enjoyed when one enters the presence of God. 'Blessed are the pure in heart: for they shall see God,' we are told in the Sermon on the Mount, although what this means, and what eternal life will be like, is not described.[5]

The best known of all the Christian prayers is the one given to his followers by Jesus himself. It is the Lord's Prayer, the 'Our Father', and in its opening line places God in heaven: 'Our Father which art in heaven, Hallowed be thy name.'[6]

If God is described as being in heaven, it surely follows that eternal life spent in the presence of God exists in a heavenly dimension, but whether heaven is a place or a state of existence is not elaborated upon.

It is not the purpose of this book to debate how a Christian is saved. The exact way in which the crucifixion is said to have redeemed us all and the interpretation of such words as 'grace' and 'salvation' is left to other writers. There is always a stream of new thinking on the age-old and eternal theme. Authors are constantly updating the implications of the crucifixion in an ever-changing world. Christians must always be prepared for those who, like the philosopher Nietzsche, declare God to be dead and comment sceptically that they would be more ready to believe in a saviour if Christians actually looked as if they had been saved.

The belief held by Christians that Jesus conquered death is also left aside for now, as is the idea that Jesus is both the lord of the living and the dead. This book has a narrower brief. What it is trying to discover are the clues as to what it is like after death. What does a person feel, experience, see, hear or discover in heaven, if it exists? Alternatively, if hell and purgatory also exist, what evidence do we have as to what those negative states of existence are like?

Trawling the New Testament for clues, several can be found, although they do not at first sight appear to point in the same direction.

The Apostle Paul suggests that believers enter into the rest of God: 'a sabbath rest still awaits the people of God', he told the Hebrews in his epistle, 'for anyone who enters God's rest, rests from his own work as God did from his. Let us then make every effort to enter that rest.'[7]

The parable, quoted earlier, of the rich man, who dressed in purple and feasted in great magnificence, and of Lazarus, the beggar who sat at his gate, may carry more than one message. In it Jesus paints a very different picture of the life to come. Luke's Gospel recounts what happened in the story when they both died. The poor man was carried away by angels to be with Abraham, while the rich man was tormented by the fires of Hades. From Hades, the rich man could see Lazarus and called out to him. Could he not just dip his finger in water and cool his tongue?[8] Can this passage be taken to be a description of the afterlife? There is no clear answer. The story is fiction; it is a parable and for a parable to be effective the storyteller has to invent characters who seem plausible and place them in situations, either mythical or real, with which listeners will be familiar. The images of the afterlife used by Jesus in the story were familiar to his listeners.

All cultures have a range of pretend places about which they talk. These never-never lands are included in traditional stories without anyone implying that the places are literally real. They are places of imagination and allegory. Today, stories are told about time travellers and spacecrafts travelling to distant galaxies, yet we know such things do not happen. When speaking of the afterlife people talk about entering heaven through the 'pearly' gates and meeting Peter with the keys.[9] It is Peter, they say, who has the power to decide who enters and who does not. The 'pearly' gate motif and the gatekeeping Peter crop up over and over again in stories, riddles and jokes:

A man was caught in a flood. Two men came by in a boat to rescue him, but he waved them away shouting, 'No, the Lord will save me.' One hour later another boat came along, but again the man said, 'No the Lord will save me.'

Eventually a helicopter arrived, but the man insisted, 'The Lord will save me.'

Unfortunately the man drowned and at the gates of heaven he asked St Peter, 'Why didn't the Lord save me?' And St Peter replied, 'For crying out loud. He sent two boats and a helicopter, what more do you want?'[10]

Employing cultural devices such as this is extremely useful to storytellers wanting to tell stories with a moral. Jesus was probably using a similar imaginary devices in giving added dramatic impact to his story of the rich man and the beggar. The details might have been made up, and the word-picture drawn from contemporary folk lore, but a world, or existence, to come was most certainly endorsed by Jesus as reality. In Matthew's Gospel he talks about the sin against the Holy Spirit which will not be forgiven, 'neither in this world, neither in the world to come'.[11] However the cautious translators of The New English Bible use the words 'either in this age or in the age to come'. That the other world, or age, will be a place, or time of purgatory is suggested by Paul in his first letter to the Corinthians. The fires of the day of judgement 'will test the worth of each man's work'.[12] But again, was he talking of every individual's day of judgement or the judgement associated with the second coming of Christ? There again perhaps the two notions of judgement, either taking place in another dimension of time, or in another dimension of space, are the same, for time in the context of eternity will no longer have the same meaning.

This understanding of time would certainly help Christians get to grips with one of the main problems in understanding the scriptural references to life after death. It is the confusion which arises as a result of the early Christians believing that the second coming and final judgement were imminent. This is illustrated by a passage in Paul's first letter to the Thessalonians:

> We want you not to remain in ignorance, brothers, about those who sleep in death; you should not grieve like the rest of men, who have no hope. We believe that Jesus died and rose again; and so it will be for those who died as Christians; God will bring them to life with Jesus.
>
> For this we tell you as the Lord's word: we who are left alive until the Lord comes shall not forestall those who have died; because at the word of command, at the sound of the archangel's voice and God's trumpet-call, the Lord himself will descend from heaven; first the Christian dead will rise, then we who are left alive shall join them, caught up in clouds to meet the Lord in the air. Thus we shall always be with the Lord.[13]

One reading of this passage suggests that Christians who are now 'asleep' in death will rise, together with Christians on earth, to join God's kingdom. We will be judged simultaneously and those who are saved will live for eternity in the presence of Jesus. Turn from Paul to the book of Revelation, the ultimate description of the end-time, and another implication is to be found that those who are saved will be limited in number to 144,000:

> On Mount Zion stood the Lamb, and with him were a hundred and forty-four thousand who had his name and the name of his Father

written on their foreheads. I heard a sound from heaven like the noise of rushing water and the deep roar of thunder; it was the sound of harpers playing on their harps. There before the throne... they were singing a new song. That song no one could learn except the hundred and forty-four thousand, who alone from the whole world had been ransomed.[14]

Yet, as with so many biblical texts, this is open to more than one interpretation and the 144,000, as the author John also implies, could be those who in the history of the world have been especially beyond reproach – the true saints. What happens to the rest? A voice from heaven tells John a little later in his vision, 'Happy are the dead who die in the faith of Christ! Henceforth... they may rest from their labours.'[15]

The raising of Christians into the air to meet the Lord, the rapture, which some Christian groups believe will be a literal phenomenon when certain individuals will suddenly vanish from the face of the earth, will only concern a limited few.

When Jesus himself talked of judgement, of parting the sheep from the goats, the sheep to his right and the goats to his left, he put no limitation on the potential numbers to be judged worthy of a place with him.[16] However he laid out the criteria for salvation and sins of omission figure highly. Rich men were almost automatically selected as goats, while innocent children were told that the kingdom of heaven belonged to them. The truly penitent were acquitted of their sins, as was the tax collector who had cheated the citizens but found remorse.[17]

Matthew's Gospel reports the words of Jesus. The metaphorical sheep, the people who are chosen, are told that they have the father's blessing: 'come, enter and possess the kingdom that has been ready for you since the world was made. For when I was hungry, you gave me food; when thirsty, you gave me drink; when I was a stranger you took me into your home, when naked you clothed me; when I was ill you came to my help, when in prison you visited me.'[18] But when, Jesus was asked, had they ministered to his needs in this way? 'I tell you this,' Jesus replied, 'anything you did for one of my brothers here, however humble, you did for me.'[19] Then come the words of judgement as the goats are told, 'The curse is upon you; go from my sight to the eternal fire that is ready for the devil and his angels.'[20] The righteous are promised eternal life; the goats are sent away to suffer eternal punishment.

The popular image of the damned going down to the fires of hell to be prodded and tormented by the demons is not backed by the words of Christ, who says that the damned will share torment with the angels of the devil, rather than be tormented by them. As the book of Revelation describes, the devil is to be 'flung into the lake of fire and sulphur, where the beast and the false prophet had been flung, there to be tormented day and night for ever'.[21]

Two verses later John writes,

I could see the dead, great and small, standing before the throne; and books were opened. Then another book was opened, the roll of the living. From what was written in these books the dead were judged upon the record of their deeds. The sea gave up its dead, and Death and Hades gave up the dead in their keeping; they were judged, each man on the record of his deeds. Then Death and Hades were flung into the lake of fire. This lake of fire is the second death; and into it were flung any whose names were not to be found in the roll of the living.[22]

It is a dramatic and awesome passage. Death and Hades are both spoken of as beings. The image of the black figure with the scythe, the grim reaper, comes to mind, as do all the other black and macabre images which have been used to portray death and which serve to fuel the flames of fear.

There is a long history of images of physical death being used to illustrate the concept of spiritual death. There are some people who revel in the ghoulish. I recall an example of this in the young woman I once met who lived entirely in the dark. In her fantasy world she believed that she was a vampire. Her bed was an ornately carved wooden coffin and all around her in her darkened house there were reminders of death. She never drew the curtains to let in the sunlight and her face was white and pale. To complete the picture of herself as a vampire she had had two of her teeth filed and she drank blood from her partner's veins.

There is a modern fashion for the Gothic which involves its followers, known as Goths, dressing entirely in black. There is a whole literature available in specialist bookshops catering for this taste in the bizarre. There are films to provide for this strange interest. Some Goths become obsessed with self-image, which appears to outsiders to be an unhealthy preoccupation.

The title of the most stomach-turning museum in the world must surely go to the one in Paris given over to the work of Jean Honoré Fragonard (1732–1806), a French painter who began to preserve human and animal cadavers for public display back in the eighteenth century. He preserved bodies in alcohol before injecting the veins and bronchial tubes with coloured wax. Fragonard was described as mad by his contemporaries, but his work survives. One visitor to the museum described a particular human exhibit in this way:

In the silent, deserted museum, his expression, his entire attitude makes it an effort of will to approach the glass of the display case. Baring his teeth beneath twisted lips and a broken nose, he looks like he is advancing towards the viewer in a fury. The veins in his heart swell blue and red… It is as though an enraged guard has caught you trying to break into the devil's sleeping quarters, and he's grabbed the first thing at hand – in this case a mandible – to ward you off. To cap the horror, a trio of human foetuses dance a macabre, ecstatic jig around his firmly planted feet. There are over a dozen other flayed figures on display in the room.[23]

One can only wonder what sort of deranged mind created such horrors. It is interesting to note that when the writer was seeking to find the words to describe the impression it made on a viewer, the name of the devil was conjured up.

The devil is the personification of evil and everything in the museum, it appears, produced in the normal viewer a sense of disgust, foreboding and evil. The fear of physical death is rooted in the dread of spiritual death, even though it is not perhaps perceived in that way. Most people shudder at the images of death and evil they see. They also find themselves curiously attracted to them. The appeal of the Chamber of Horrors at Madame Tussaud's Wax Museum, or Hammer Horror films, lies in this ambivalence. Evil often has a strange lure. And people find themselves reluctantly drawn towards the temptations of the macabre. It is part of the age-old struggle between good and evil, right and wrong, which Christians would say exists inside every human being. It is a struggle which can perhaps become resolved by facing up to the macabre and not hiding from it. The day of the dead celebrated in Latin America takes the form of a carnival in which people dress as corpses, skeletons and images of death and express their deepest fears in flamboyant merrymaking.

Many people of faith, however, have lost the fear of death, as the struggle inside them between good and evil became more and more one-sided, with good triumphing. The words uttered by martyrs, both ancient and modern, and the testimony of their final acts illustrates convincingly that they believed in a life to come, but had little idea what to expect. Before his execution at the hands of the Nazis, the German Lutheran pastor Dietrich Bonhoeffer prayed:

> Do with me according to your will,
>   and as is best for me.
> Whether I live or die, I am with you,
>   and you, my God, are with me.
> Lord, I wait for your salvation
>   and for your kingdom.[24]

And those who are never tested to the extreme, but who live normal lives and are faced with normal-sized temptations can also develop a healthy view of death: 'Dying is like a boy's voice breaking and his putting on trews, or like a young girl and she letting down the hem of her skirt and putting up her soft hair... We are like childer on the floor and the dead are grown up.'[25] Or, as the elderly Pope John XXIII put it before his death, 'My bags are packed, I am ready to go.'[26]

I know one remarkable woman, now in her nineties, yet full of mental vigour and delight in life, who accepts that death is just round the corner. She is unconcerned as she has a total belief in the afterlife. Without hesitation or embarrassment she says she knows that a place awaits her in heaven. She attributes her certainty to the faith of her father, an Anglican clergyman. The words of Jesus in John's Gospel ring entirely true to her, as they do to so many other Christians: 'And if I go and prepare a place for you, I will come again, and receive you unto myself; that where I am, there ye may be also.'[27]

In one commentary on the words of John, the commentator writes of the love of Jesus, the servant king, who prepares a place in eternity 'for the likes of you and me'. She continues, 'I have been with people who have died in faith, in sure and certain hope of God's promises being fulfilled: some of them have died with the "light of heaven" in their faces. Some seem actually to have seen their dear departed, before they've breathed their last.'[28]

Yet the words of Jesus are, when read in context, enigmatic. In the same chapter of John's Gospel he goes on to say that, while he is the way to the Father in heaven, the Father also dwells inside us: 'because I live, you too will live; then you will know that I am in my Father, and you in me and I in you'.[29] The implication is that the thing we see as death is not a barrier to God. The love of God is available before death and after death. It is available on earth and in the life beyond. Spiritual life, eternal life, can begin in this earthly life and continue after physical death. It is a clear indication in the gospels that spiritual death and physical death are not the same, even though the images of physical death might be employed to create fears of spiritual death.

To those of faith it is utterly reassuring, yet it still gives no indication as to what spiritual life in the state beyond physical death is actually like, although many Christians will say, so what? If we are assured that spiritual life continues, let's keep the details as a surprise! God is after all a God of surprises.

CHAPTER SEVEN

Looking Death in the Face

When the Roman Catholic leader Cardinal Basil Hume learned that he had inoperable cancer he made a dignified and low-key announcement of the fact to his clergy. The news quickly spread to the laity in his church and to the nation as a whole. He was near to death, he said, but he hoped to survive the year. The timing of his illness, he acknowledged openly, was in the hands of God. He expressed no fear of death, although he must have had some anxiety about the manner of his dying. The last weeks of cancer can be particularly unpleasant if the palliative care is not gauged correctly.

It is often said that the vocation of a monk is to prepare for death, and so a simple statement of the inevitable, and his faithful acceptance of the inevitable, was what one would have expected from a man who, although a prelate of the church, remained a Benedictine religious at heart. Yet his announcement was not just one of fact, it was also a challenge. The challenge was directed at the secular world. Today in Britain, and generally in the Western world, for someone to face their own end with tranquillity and acceptance runs counter to the prevailing culture. Cardinal Hume wanted his final message to be one of hope. He wished to make as public a statement as possible that he believed death was not the end, rather a new beginning.

In approaching death with tranquillity, and in not wanting the medical profession to do all in its power to delay the inevitable, Cardinal Hume was among the minority of patients facing the slow but inevitable process of dying. In sharp contrast with Cardinal Hume we have the word-picture created by the Welsh poet Dylan Thomas, from the angry and desperate poem written at the time of the death of his father:

> Do not go gentle into that good night,
> Old age should burn and rave at close of day;
> Rage, rage against the dying of the light.[1]

Yet, slowly, assumptions and attitudes are changing. Death, the taboo subject, is now edging its way out of the closet. More people are being prepared to talk about their approaching deaths without anger and bitterness. Several high-profile writers have used and are using their own experiences of terminal illness to explore and confront common feelings and fears. One British journalist has written a weekly column describing in minute detail his medical progress and his feelings as cancer takes over his life and body.[2] The hospice movement is also proactive in saying that the process of dying can be medically managed and that no one need spend their final days or weeks in distress of either mind or body.

Sadly, even with the knowledge accumulated by the hospice movements, patients continue to die in pain.

'The godlike consultant gave my father two options: bilateral amputation above the knee, or slow death by toxaemia and gangrene, sending my father insane,'[3] wrote a friend of Valerie Grove in a letter to the Times journalist. The dying man, an octogenarian, was a patient in a hospital near Glasgow. His daughter sat with him through harrowing days and nights during which he bellowed in agony. She described the public and humiliating manner in which his pleas were ignored during ward rounds:

His mental pain easily matched his physical pain. Eventually, a sympathetic night nurse got his pain under control. But the mental anguish remained, breaking through intermittently and heart-breakingly as he begged for release. Only at the end, when I had threatened to take matters into my own hands, was a palliative-care specialist sent for, who administered the drugs I requested.[4]

A wide range of issues relating to death is starting to be raised through the media of television and popular culture in a way it would not have been tackled a few years ago. These issues even venture into some difficult areas of ethics. How far should relatives go to keep a dying person alive? Is a shorter life of high quality better than an extended life of low quality?

The storyline of an episode of the UK television drama series *The Bill* followed the case of a couple raising money to take their terminally ill child to America. They believed that it was the only place in the world whose medical treatment offered them hope. In the end they decided that the distress which would be caused to their daughter in pursuing a 5-per-cent chance of life would be too much for her, and that an acceptance of her death was the kinder option, and the one in her best interests. They decided to remain at home and devote themselves to making the last months of their child's life as happy as possible.[5]

Three or four generations ago death was far more widely discussed and accepted. The impression that comes down to us from the Victorian era in Britain is of a society which was not only familiar with natural death, but also revelled in the sentimentality of it. It was a way of coping with the frequency of infant and maternal death. Families were large. The sentimentality of the times accounted for the popularity of such fictional characters as Dickens' Little Nell who took an unconscionable time dying in his story, *The Old Curiosity Shop*.

While attitudes towards death might be undergoing change, there remains a huge public ignorance of death in the developed world. While we all become acquainted with death, as friends and relations die, we tend to keep the realities of dying at arms' length. Dealing with death first-hand is a matter left to the professionals – ambulance crews, doctors, pathologists, mortuary attendants, undertakers and so on.

Death, however, is ever present in entertainment and in the news, even though it remains absent from most people's everyday experience. As a result many people think they know, but few of them actually know, what happens when death occurs. Contrary to the impression left by the mass media, the majority of deaths are not the result of violence. Only a small percentage of deaths are attributable to murder, ethnic cleansing or bomb blasts. Most people die of natural causes – heart disease or cancer. Even during the First World War, that most notorious and bloody of modern conflicts, which took place between 1914 and 1918 in Europe, the major cause of death was not trench warfare, but the usual range of common diseases, including those no longer considered to be generally life-threatening such as measles and influenza.

Most deaths are not an unnatural termination of life, but life's natural conclusion, however early or late the conclusion might come. A death can even be a satisfying, purposeful and fulfilling experience to all involved, as this account of the passing of a friend testifies.

The island of Fetlar in Shetland is a bleak and stormy place for most of the winter. It is the home, however, to a small community of religious sisters who both survive and thrive in the harsh weather conditions. The community, the Society of Our Lady of the Isles, was founded several years ago by Mother Mary Agnes, supported and encouraged by her friend Rosemary, a retired teacher of disabled children. In January 1999, just four weeks after the shortest day, Rosemary lay dying. Mary Agnes sat by her bedside keeping watch. The window was slightly open and to her surprise the sound of birdsong drifted into the room: 'The winter up here has its own, often violent, symphonies of sound,' Mary Agnes was to write later, 'though for me they have never included such an outpouring as that of that tiny lark singing its heart out. I squeezed Rosemary's hand and asked if she could hear it and she nodded.'[6] The moment brought to her mind an occasion many years earlier when Mary Agnes had been a member of a community in Devon and she had sat with a fellow sister through her last moments on this earth:

> On this occasion it was in the early hours of the morning, moments after she had passed away. I had just returned to my cell from her bedside and I became aware of the beautiful and unforgettable strains of the nightingale. In the darkness I leaned on the narrow windowsill and was transfixed by the melody... It is said that birds are God's harbinger of heaven; that they are the tiny heralds who welcome God's beloved ones home.[7]

It is an indisputable fact that every one of us alive today will sooner or later die. Death might come tomorrow or it might be deferred for many more years. It might come in a violent form – tragically and prematurely – or, more likely, it will come at the end of a good, faithful, eventful, chaotic, imperfect, wasted or useful life.

Like every birth and every life, every death is unique, as was emphasized earlier. There is no textbook on how to die. Rosemary died a few hours after the lark had sung for her. Her death did not cast a shadow of gloom over the community. On the contrary, Mother Mary Agnes spoke of a tangible feeling of joy, peace and fulfilment which encompassed those who were left. The day of her funeral was a day of celebration. She was buried in the kirk yard on the island and, since her birthday had been 11 November, her friends threw red poppies of remembrance into her grave.

Three weeks later, and 800 miles away, a funeral took place at a West London crematorium. The chapel was full to capacity with friends, relations and schoolmates who were there to say goodbye to Molly, who had died at the age of fourteen.

Molly had almost died at birth and, because of her disabling physical condition, was never expected to have a full life. For her mother Lesley every day of Molly's life had been a bonus. She was a gifted, witty child with a sense of fun and maturity beyond her years and feeble body, who once said of herself, 'I've got a brain that works and a body that doesn't.'[8] Her funeral was not a religious ceremony, but a series of tributes from those who knew her – prose and poetry:

> How is Molly? asks Angus
> The day after she died.
> I pause and say, She's dead.
> A pause from him before he says
> She's not doing very well then.
> How is Molly? asks Tommy too.
> And Angus again, the next night.
> I give the same reply.
> Don't they understand,
> Or don't I?

For someone who was physically so slight and fragile, the chasm which her death leaves is gigantic.

> mystery
> for reason to stand in awe and surely stand down.

Molly was alright. That's the point. That's what she taught me. Molly was teaching us things from the very beginning. She was happy. And she was affable: her own description. She was content. And she certainly enjoyed herself.

> I heard a tiny voice…
> It was linked to a smile
> And a head of straight gold hair
> And penetrating quizzical eyes

Magnified by spectacles.
In the future
If I am fortunate
And I listen closely,
I hope to hear a tiny voice
Not above or beyond,
But sewn within
The ambient din of life.

And there was this contribution from ten-year-old Samuel Levin which began with five questions:

Why did she have to die?
Why do people have to die?
Why do they die of any problems?
Why can't they live to become old aged?
Why do people have to die?
Why did she have to die?

A few months later, at the end of the summer term, her friends held another gathering to remember Molly. They gathered in the school hall and some of Molly's artwork was on display, as were photographs of her. It was not a religious service. There was no priest. Music was played, both live on a piano, and on record. It was music Molly had related to in life and included a strangely haunting composition by the Australian cult performer, poet and songwriter, Nick Cave. To the background of a repetitive piano phrase, Cave's words filled the hall. It was an expression of both compromise and ambivalence in matters of faith and seemed very appropriate:

I don't believe in an interventionist God,
But I know darling that you do.
If I did I would kneel down and ask him

Not to intervene when it came to you.
Not to touch a hair on your head,
Leave you as you are.
But if he felt he had to direct you,
To direct you into my arms.
Into my arms, Oh Lord, into my arms.[9]

Neither Molly's nor Rosemary's deaths had been unexpected. The teenage girl and the retired teacher, despite living for very different lengths of time, had both lived to their full capacity for joy and this was reflected in the way they were remembered and celebrated. For those who knew Rosemary her parting was celebrated as an expression of the joy to be found by her friends and community in their faith in Christ. For those who knew Molly, they recalled the joy of times past when Molly had been at the centre of their laughter and delight in life.

Maybe facing death is hardest for those who are left behind whose happy recall is always tempered by the realization that those remembered days will never return, except in memory. Whatever happens after death, for the person who experiences the joys or the oblivion of it, the questions are either all answered or past needing to be asked.

This idea was presented formally at a funeral held in a country church in Kent in the summer of the same year as the funerals of Molly and Rosemary. It was for a respected philosopher who in life had had little time for glib or sloppy thinking on spiritual matters. A reading was given from *The Apology* by Plato:

Death is one of two things. Either it is annihilation, and the dead have no consciousness of anything; or, as we are told, it is really a change: a migration of the soul from this place to another. Now if there is no consciousness but only a dreamless sleep, death must be a marvellous gain. I suppose that if anyone were told to pick out the night on which he slept so soundly as not even to dream, and then were told to say how many better and happier days and nights than this he had spent in the course of his life – well I think that the Great King himself would find these days and nights easy to count.

If on the other hand death is a removal from here to some other place, and if what we are told is true, that all the dead are there, what greater blessing could there be than this? If on arrival in the other world, one finds there are... all those half-divinities who were upright in their earthly life, would that be an unrewarding journey?

I am willing to die ten times over if this account is true. Because apart from the other happiness in which their world surpasses ours, they are now immortal for the rest of time.[10]

This attractive approach to the conundrum of the afterlife contains its own internal logic and peculiar brand of comfort. But it is an approach which requires to be read with a certain detachment to be convincing. Those mourners who are utterly absorbed by the emotions of grief and departing find such semantics leave them cold. It is the uncomprehending school-friend, the mother taking her leave of the child she brought into the world, who feel the pain of separation most strongly.

Why did she, or he, have to die? is the universal question of the human condition. It is the question which reoccurs time after time in life as one's own friends age and depart this earth. It is perhaps the asking of this question which distinguishes humans from other animals. It is thought that other species grieve, but there is no suggestion that abstract questions arise out of that grief.

The question, Why is there death? is of course the reverse of the question, Why is there life? The two questions are interdependent and cannot exist alone. They are at the root of the quest for faith, for the journey of faith is the search for purpose. The questions are also the introduction to mystery and it is through the exploration of mystery that a sense of the numinous may be experienced.

'*Cogito, ergo sum*,' wrote Réne Descartes more than three centuries ago – 'I think, therefore I am.'[11] We are conscious beings and one of the burdens of consciousness is that it has an unsettling and questing nature. It demands to comprehend itself and know if it exists merely as a freak and ephemeral consequence of evolution, or whether it is evidence that the universe exists for a reason and a purpose. The prevailing secular view teaches that as human beings we are products of chance. We have evolved and adapted into our present purposeless form and simply exist for an infinitesimal blip of geological time. Ultimately the chemicals of our bodies will be randomly reformed into new arrangements of matter. Given that perspective on the human race it is no wonder that death is a subject best not discussed or acknowledged.

However, we are all egocentric beings who find it hard to accept that we are just blobs of valueless matter. There is a special comfort in the idea that we are created in the image of a God who loves us each individually and infinitely. Are we just deluding ourselves when we think along these lines?

Only after death might we know more. Death may thus be seen as a gateway to knowledge. But viewed from here, from this world, from the perspective of those watching by the deathbed, it is nothing of the kind. Death involves parting, suffering, grieving and ultimately decomposition and decay. There is no irrefutable indication given at the moment of death to suggest that anything of the person survives the last breath. Conversely, there is no evidence found in death to prove conclusively that nothing lies beyond. Perhaps death is an initiation and it is only by each one of us walking through the valley of the shadow of death that we can emerge from that shadow into the light of knowledge.

'Dying can be seen not merely as the end of life', wrote Marion Stroud, 'but as a very special phase of personal growth and development.'[12] Yet it is not a phase most people enter willingly and even those with the strongest faith enter the phase apprehensively. If life is pleasant and death promises to be peaceful, that does not mean the transition from one to the other will not be bumpy.

As well as being a period of pain, discomfort and loss of dignity and control, dying can be a time of doubt. The celebrated preacher David Watson, who died of cancer, told of the dark, lonely small hours of the night:

The worst times for me were at 2 or 3 o'clock in the morning. I had preached... all over the world with ringing conviction. I had told countless thousands of people that I was not afraid of death since through Christ I had already received God's gift of eternal life. For years I had not doubted these truths at all. But now the fundamental questions were nagging away... If I was soon on my way to heaven, how real was heaven? Was it anything more than a beautiful idea? What honestly would happen when I died? Did God himself really exist after all? How could I be sure? Indeed how could I be certain of anything apart from cancer and death?... Never before had my faith been so ferociously attacked.[13]

In a way his experience was like that of Jesus in the garden of Gethsemane. He was left alone to suffer his doubts and misgivings. David Watson died despite the fervent prayers of his supporters and members of his congregation. They must have felt a little like the disciples after the crucifixion. Their faith was severely tested by what seemed to them to be God ignoring their requests. One way in which Christians can understand the way in which Christ conquered death is by considering how he shared the same doubts and loneliness in the course of facing his own physical death.

Following her extensive study of the dying process through her many conversations with patients at the point of death, Elisabeth Kübler-Ross identified a pattern of emotions frequently experienced as death approaches inexorably. She undertook her research in the 1960s in Chicago, but her observations have wide application. Her research technique was simple. She asked patients who were beyond medical help to describe to her the experience of dying as it happened. She identified a five-stage process starting with denial, going through anger, bargaining and depression until reaching a point of acceptance.

She also noted the importance of hope. This did not necessarily mean hope of a cure, although sometimes that was the hope patients harboured, but hope that there was a purpose to dying, that dying would give an opportunity to seek reconciliation with friends and family, or hope in a life to come. Her comment that once a patient stops expressing hope it is usually a sign of imminent death may be seen as applying to both the material and the spiritual hope.

Kübler-Ross was not without her critics and later writers like Kathleen Dowling Singh have suggested that her five-stage theory requires clarification and revision:

> Each of the mental and emotional reactions of the five-stage theory of dying is a reaction of the mental ego forced to confront the death of the body in which it presumes itself to reside… Evidence accumulated from increased interaction with people who are dying now suggests that the stages of dying involve psychospiritual transformations deep into transpersonal levels; in fact, perhaps, all the way to Unity Consciousness.[14]

Unity Consciousness, as described by Kathleen Dowling Singh, is that state in which the person is beyond their ego-bound self – to employ the technical language of the psychotherapist. It may also be said to mean God-realization. It involves finding a sense of the numinous which is normally beyond us in life. It seems that she is arguing that in the course of dying, before the final breath is expired, the person has already caught glimpses of the afterlife.

Elisabeth Kübler-Ross was herself transformed by her participation with the powerful catalyst of death, observing that for those who seek to understand it, death is a highly creative force. The highest spiritual values of life can originate from the thought and study of death. In all this it must not be forgotten that Kübler-Ross was, in her work, looking at natural death. Traumatic death and victim death produce very different responses in those who witness them. To people unused to seeing suffering and gore, the events might become burned on their minds in such a way as to cause long-term disturbance. Post-traumatic stress disorder is now widely acknowledged to be a long-lasting effect suffered by those who have seen, or been involved in, wars or major accidents. Also death seen through the tears of grief may present a very different picture.

But can there also be an overfamiliarity with death? Are the death professionals liable to become hardened to it and treat it ultimately with indifference or contempt? There are certainly many individuals who, despite their work, remain remarkably balanced and sensitive in the face of daily contact with death. Only when the deaths are particularly revolting or needless does anger threaten to subsume their reason. Many who work in the emergency services will probably say that they have little time to contemplate the spiritual opportunities presented by the demands on their skills and training, yet they seem not to be untouched by the spirituality of what they do.

The death professionals are often people of quiet faith who, as well as giving hope to those who feel abandoned as they face death, also unwittingly draw strength from people of faith who turn their own deaths into positive experiences. While they daily help others face the end, they view the process as part of the wider experience of life and of God's purpose.

Yet deep and disturbing questions must arise in the minds of the professionals and it is dangerous to avoid them. If the questions are allowed to fester too long, or disturbing issues left suppressed, they are likely to rise to the surface when least expected and least wanted. The policeman who deals with the body of a murdered child, the fireman who removes the charred corpses of a family from a house which has been deliberately set on fire, come face to face with the consequences of evil.

The existence of evil in the world is one of the imponderables. It is even difficult to define evil, except in the negative. It is that which exists in contradiction to goodness and love. Evil cannot be isolated. It is not an absolute state. It can only exist in relation to good. Every one of us is a blend of good and evil, right and wrong. There can be individual evil and corporate evil. Collectively people can sanction actions which individually they would never contemplate. This happens particularly at times of war, but also happens on a day-to-day basis. If we buy goods in a supermarket which have been produced by exploited cheap labour, we are endorsing an evil. Yet if, for instance, we buy flowers produced by child-labour in South America, and give them as a gesture of love to someone in hospital, good and evil get very confused.

The nature of evil makes for fascinating study, but it may be thought to be a study somewhat at a tangent to the main purpose of this book. Yet it should not be overlooked that evil, direct or indirect, is a factor in the cause of many unnatural or premature deaths. In an extreme form the evil of Nazism resulted in the millions of deaths of the Second World War and the Holocaust.

But does the cause of death affect what happens to a person after death? That is not something readily knowable. However it can be observed that the cause of a death and the circumstances surrounding it certainly affect the witnesses' perception of death. A police officer who finds the body of an abused child will be revolted by what he or she has to deal with. Nightmares might follow as a form of post-traumatic stress disorder occurs. The horror of the evil might taint that person's life for a long time. However, the death and the cause of the death can be separated out and a picture of a victim at rest need not always be overshadowed by the picture of how the victim met his or her end. Even in extreme cases this can be true. Court officials and police investigators who had to listen to the taped cries of the moors murders victims will never forget the harrowing sounds or the evil that was at work will never be forgotten, yet the children who died, it must also be remembered are suffering no more. Christians will be sure that they are safely in the care of a loving God.

A person may be at peace with death unless it is the case that somehow a person's final moments are those which get frozen in eternity. This is a fantasy notion for which there is no evidence, but, like the horrors of being buried alive, a very real concern to those who have it. The idea is that the last image or feeling experienced in life is the one frozen for eternity. Thus a person who dies content remains content in the afterlife; the person who is troubled at the moment of death remains an eternally troubled soul. Hearing is said to be the last sense which fades with death and there is a common belief in Islam that if the name of God is uttered in a dying person's ear it helps the soul reach heaven.

It is of comfort to those who think this way that the body itself has its own mechanism to induce a feeling of peace at the end. Victims of murder, however horrific their end, would presumably get a shot of endorphins in the final moments – in much the same way as Dr Livingstone described when ambushed by a hungry lion – or drift into unconsciousness. In citing the case of a victim murdered by a paranoid schizophrenic, Sherwin Nuland makes a strong claim that the victim's last moments were peaceful. She was repeatedly stabbed in front of witnesses. Her face and neck were hacked by a knife. Her mother described how she rushed forward to take her daughter in her arms when the assailant was eventually pulled away:

> There was no look of pain in her eyes, but instead it was a look of surprise. And then... her eyes glazed over... I thought Kate is not in her body anymore. She's behind me, up there above me, floating. Her face showed confusion... not a look of horror. She must have released herself from the pain, because her face didn't show it.[15]

Nuland commented, 'I am convinced that nature stepped in and provided exactly the right spoonful of medicine to give a measure of tranquillity to a dying child.'

Conversely, those who meet their deaths as a consequence of the evil they have done might find death brings with it a very different experience. Executed criminals go to their deaths in the expectation that they will have their guilt lying heavily on their consciences. There are many reports of criminals finding forgiveness at the time of their execution and who go to their maker in peace. However, others go to the gallows or the electric chair defiant to the end, consumed with hatred against both the legal system and themselves.

If, as is reported by many who have undergone near-death experiences, part of the final process of life is that the brain is filled with a rapid play-through of the past, then the moment of death is a significant one. It is said that at death one's life flashes before one's eyes. The dying murderer will, therefore, see much with which to reproach himself, but even then, perhaps can find time for remorse and forgiveness. Who, in this final moment on earth, seeing themselves as they really have been, could fail to feel ashamed or guilty about some of their past deeds?

Judgement appears in various dramatic forms in ancient texts on dying including *The Egyptian Book of the Dead* and the medieval Christian work, *Ars Moriendi* (*The Craft of Dying*). In *Ars Moriendi*, the writer, not believing in reincarnation, emphasized the need for confession and death of egotistical desires before coming into the presence of God and that spiritual counselling should take place as the person is approaching the end.[16] 'The state of mind of the dying person', says Sandol Stoddard, 'is of utmost importance to his ultimate destiny.'[17]

Some traditions would take the proposition further and argue that the dying person must take an initiative in dying well. The Dalai Lama talks of the importance of the dying person staying aware. 'As much as you are aware, so much greater is the capacity to remember the previous life after rebirth.'[18]

Plato observed that philosophy was a rehearsal for death. By contemplating one's mortality, death can become a familiar companion. *The Tibetan Book of the Dead* suggests using the imagination to dissolve out of the body into realms of pure light: 'Let go, gently, gently without the least force. Before you shines your true being. It is without birth, without death. Let go of all which distracts or confuses the mind… Do not pull back in fear from the immensity of your true being.'[19]

Another description of a rehearsal for death instructs the participant to close the eyes and imagine being on a deathbed. The body has no energy left to attend to the practical things of life. They no longer matter. 'There is only one thing to do and that is let go… Shed the heavy loads… of self-importance… do it with care, do it with love.'[20]

These ideas, which can be relevant to people of many faiths, brings us back to the difference between physical death and spiritual death. What matters at the end, perhaps, is not the final image of life, but the spiritual condition of the dying person. Is he or she agitated and wanting to hang on to the small things of life, or is the person willing and ready to let go and, in Christian terms, commend their spirit to the love of God? If spiritual life survives physical death, then the state of the spiritual life at the point of physical death is what matters in the next life. On one hand, a person who is so consumed with evil that they are spiritually dead is perhaps the one destined for eternity to be separated from the love of God. On the other hand, people executed for their faith, in other words the martyrs of history, are believed to die with the absolute certainty in their minds that they are destined for eternal reward.

In many hagiographies of martyrs their deaths are given special heroic qualities. Legends develop about dramatic events at the end, or famous last words. One martyred bishop, Polycarp of Smyrna, was burned alive around AD 155:

He uttered a prayer of praise and Glory to God and when he had offered himself and said Amen, the fire was kindled. The flames made a sort of arch, like a ship's sail filled with the wind, and they were like a wall round the martyr's body; and he looked, not like burning flesh, but like bread in the oven or gold and silver being refined in a furnace. Then the executioner was ordered to stab Polycarp to hasten his end.[21]

The bravery of Thomas Becket, archbishop of Canterbury, in facing his murder at the hands of the king's knights fuelled legends which resulted in his canonization and the development of a cult and pilgrimage tradition which lasted several centuries.

It is, of course, speculation to seek to divide death into its two components, physical and spiritual, but it makes some sense of the persistent belief in so many cultures that life beyond can take one of two directions – a path to paradise or a path to Hades.

CHAPTER EIGHT

Preparing, Planning and Thwarting

It is often said today of someone who dies unexpectedly, 'At least he went quickly: he didn't know anything about it.' Even many churchgoers talk about a good death as dying in one's sleep before one is aware of what is happening. It is not a sentiment our ancestors would have recognized. The Litany, now little used in the Church of England, but still part of the official Book of Common Prayer, contains the verse: 'From lightning and tempest; from plague, pestilence, and famine; from battle and murder, and from sudden death, Good Lord deliver us.'

As Elisabeth Kübler-Ross found, people who approach death gradually and fully aware of what is happening go through five stages of psychological preparation. The sixteenth-century writer of the Litany would also have been familiar with the idea of preparing for death, even if he would not have expressed it in the same twentieth-century manner. Indeed the compiler of The Book of Common Prayer, Archbishop Cranmer, had plenty of time to prepare for his death. He was burned at the stake in Oxford in 1556. He expressed his remorse, as the flames took hold, that he had been tempted to renounce his principles.

A sudden death by pestilence or murder was one which gave little or no room for preparation. Thus legal and secular affairs as well as spiritual concerns were in danger of being left in disarray. Preparing for death in a practical way is therefore encouraged by those seeking to help the dying.

When Sir Leonard Cheshire, VC, the founder of the Cheshire Homes (originally for people disabled by war and now catering for a wider range of people with disabilities) and celebrated hero of the Second World War, learned that he was dying of motor neurone disease, he dictated an account of his spiritual preparations. At first he had to adjust for the loss of movement and physical health, having enjoyed a life of action. Then he emptied his mind of anything self-centred and took the opportunity of offering up that which he was losing as a gift to someone else.[1] Offering one's suffering is a spiritual discipline often practised within the Roman Catholic Church, of which Sir Leonard was a member. Mother Teresa founded a team of co-workers who were ill or housebound who offered their suffering and prayers to help her team of sisters. I once met one of her co-workers, a woman crippled with arthritis living in a tower block in London. She was linked in prayer to an Indian sister. They corresponded and took strength from each other.

Sir Leonard's second career had been devoted to helping others. In his third career, that of suffering, he described how he found joy in sharing the disabilities he had previously only known second-hand. He founded the Family of the Cross for people who wished to follow the contemplative life, but who could not join a religious community because of illness. As his own illness progressed he contrived to find a new sense of happiness. 'It is seldom that one reads about anyone so obviously carrying out the purpose for which they were created,' wrote one reviewer.[2]

There is a clear distinction which must be drawn, however, between preparation and planning. Planning involves arranging the death itself and enters into the tragic area of suicide and the contentious area of euthanasia. (Perhaps in this context I should be more specific and say voluntary euthanasia. Compulsory euthanasia, as practised by a society wishing to rid itself of those members it perceives as burdensome, is a form of eugenics and not the issue here.)

Making adequate preparations, in a practical sense, is often part of the spiritual preparation. It might involve making plans for the welfare of dependents, or making a will to ensure that the estate left is equitably distributed. It could also take the form of drawing up a blueprint for the funeral. It might involve recording thoughts and memories from which future generations might learn or derive pleasure.

The subject of suicide is one which needs to be raised. At one stage in British legal history it was a criminal offence to commit suicide. For 1,500 years it was also taught by the church that it was a sin so severe that it could result in only one thing – eternal damnation. Every suicide is an individual and desperate act, but trying to analyse the reasons why some people take their own lives is not the brief of this book. Our questions about suicide are more specific and they are to do with what happens afterwards.

In this context it is worth remembering that it was not until the sixth century that Christians took the view that suicide was wrong. In some societies, including that of ancient Rome and Greece, suicide could sometimes be viewed as an honourable and dignified way to die. In modern Japan suicide is still seen as a way of extracting honour from humiliation. In many parts of the world old people who feel that they are a burden to their families withdraw from life. They might refuse to take food and water, or wander alone into the desert or bush to find a quiet spot to sit and wait for their end. A friend of mine on his return from a trek across Africa once told me how he had found human remains in a remote spot through which he had walked. He reported the fact to villagers in the next settlement who appeared unconcerned. They knew whose remains they were. They were of an old lady who had felt the time had come to die.

The change in the Christian attitude to suicide is attributed to the early Christians' enthusiasm for martyrdom. There is only a narrow definition to separate those who volunteer for martyrdom and those who initiate their own death. Martyrs, so Christians believe, have their sins forgiven and win themselves a place in heaven.

There are some who kill themselves because they are so desperately unhappy or disturbed in this life that they seek oblivion. If after suicide oblivion is achieved, they will have found their rest. In the Cheyenne culture of North America it is believed that suicide is the way to guarantee oblivion. The Cheyenne believe those who commit suicide are diverted on their way to dwell alongside God and are dispatched to a state of nothingness.

In some cases suicide is a sign of impatience with life. The members of the Heaven's Gate cult, who committed suicide en masse, did so to speed themselves on their way to a new life – or so they believed. There was also the puzzling case of the suicide of the priest who had once been a member of the exclusive Special Air Service, and who in his army days had taken a leading role in the relief of the Iranian Embassy siege. Revd Frank Collins remained the action man, even when ordained. It appeared that he had everything to live for yet, at the age of forty-one, he took his own life. He left four children.

The suicide was planned, so it appeared, with military precision. He fixed a vacuum cleaner hose to the exhaust of a car and ran the pipe to the rear window. He sat in the car in a friend's garage, started the engine and began reading *War and Peace* by torchlight. He was found dead the next morning, poisoned by the carbon monoxide from the exhaust.

A coroner later heard a range of evidence to try to fathom why Frank Collins had committed suicide. Newspaper reporters also tried to find the reason when they spoke to Frank's family and friends. One suggestion made, which appears to make some sense, was that Frank had no fear of death. He had seen it first-hand. He was a man eager and restless for adventure and possibly viewed death as the final mission. Was he impatient to get started? Did he, as one friend suggested, view death as the ultimate adventure. He had no doubts about an afterlife, said another friend, he just couldn't wait to get there. It is not a view his family share.

No one will ever know the facts, but if it was the case that he died to satisfy his curiosity and impatience, then it was a highly selfish act. It was wrong. But whether the same argument can be applied in different circumstances, perhaps to a loner with no responsibilities, is a different matter. If an old person with nothing left to live for decides to seek death a few months early, is that wrong? Some suicides can be described as altruistic. When Captain Oates, on the return journey from the South Pole with Captain Scott, felt that his injuries were hindering his companions' chance of survival, he walked out into the snow to die.

If suicide is a sin, some Christians will want to know if dying when committing a sin immediately consigns the soul to hell. After the death of Diana, Princess of Wales, one minister suggested that as she was driving on her way to commit adultery, she would have been consigned to eternal damnation. There was an angry response to the suggestion. It was not what her millions of supporters wanted to hear, but it had a logic to it.

In the Roman Catholic tradition confession, if genuine, and absolution at the end are said to wipe the slate clean. If, however, a person dies robbing a bank, swearing, telling a lie or driving too fast, or by their own hand, or quite by chance but in the middle of an unworthy thought, what then? A few more years in purgatory? The gospels suggest that one should live each day as if it is the last.[3] It is good practical advice whether one expects to die imminently or not. It is advice, of course, which appears to contradict the common-sense approach to life: one should save for a rainy day and make sensible preparations for old age or even, in the short run, make sure there is food in the house for the weekend's meals.

The various conundra point relentlessly back to the same conclusion: if spiritual death and physical death are disengaged from each other, then the practical concerns about material life need not contradict the practical concerns about spiritual life. This division of death into its two components can only make sense to a person who has a belief in the spiritual realm. To me it is one of the puzzles of the debate that those who have no belief in a spiritual afterlife are most often those who are prepared to sanction the foreshortening of life.

Yet advocates of voluntary euthanasia are frequently those with no notion of a life to come. A typical view was expressed by Jean Davies of the Voluntary Euthanasia Society when she wrote, 'When we die that is the end of us. It will be exactly like being asleep or unconscious without ever waking up. As far as I am concerned after my death will be the same experience as before my conception, i.e. nothingness… I certainly would not want to live for ever.'[4]

It might be supposed that it would be the people with no hope of anything beyond the grave who would cling on to life. Yet the opposite is true. Maybe the thought of going to sleep after a long and troublesome illness and never waking up is appealing. Perhaps the explanation is to be found in the belief commonly held that every human being has a right to determine his or her own destiny. If the last few weeks of life are to be painful and degrading and, by definition, pointless and frustrating, why not decide for oneself when to die? We choose the way we live, why should we not also choose the way we die? There is a logic to that if the spiritual possibilities are removed from the equation. To extend the philosophical debate the question can be asked, What are rights? If they are grounded in moral obligations, then on what does society base its code of morality if there is no religion?

If, however, it is believed that it might be possible to grow spiritually as a result of suffering, and that as physical life declines so spiritual life increases, then cutting short life might be counterproductive. Except that it can be argued that if spiritual life follows death, why not hasten its arrival, as perhaps Frank Collins did, but with less justification than someone in acute pain? That, however, takes a further factor out of consideration – God. If God is the creator of everything, including our physical self, do we have the right to destroy that which God made? Or, as some Christians might argue, if God has planned that we die in a

162

certain way, should we thwart his wishes? 'Thy will, not mine,' as Christians are taught to pray.

The problem with answering that question concerning the will of God is this: by the time a person is near physical death, the physical self, the body, made by God is nothing like the original model. It has been ravaged by illness and disease and possibly by the after-effects of the sins of the flesh! The drinker's diseased liver is the work of a creator God largely altered by the free will and excesses of the owner.

The knee-jerk reaction of many Christians against voluntary euthanasia is not as easy to justify on religious grounds as one might suppose. The real argument against deliberately ending a human life, as one might put a pet cat or dog to sleep, surely lies in the word 'voluntary'. Can it ever be guaranteed that a person whose life is to be ended by a medically prescribed fatal dose has given willing consent? How might a law permitting voluntary euthanasia be manipulated by unscrupulous relatives or even hard-pressed governments looking to save money on the budget set aside for the care of the elderly?

When David Alton, the parliamentarian, argued strongly against the introduction of a bill to permit voluntary euthanasia he challenged the financial arguments in favour. He feared that doctors and health administrators would find the premature ending of life a cheap option. And certainly when it is considered that the majority of money spent on healthcare on an individual is in the final year of life, and that many important life-prolonging treatments are not available through lack of money, the financial arguments in favour of euthanasia are attractive. 'The flaws in this silver-tongued argument', wrote David Alton, 'revolve around then questions of consent, the commissioning of doctors and nurses as killers, and the fundamental questions of life itself. There is a clear line between killing and letting die. Care and kill cannot be used as synonyms.'[5]

One possible way of controlling potential abuses is through living wills. A living will is the opportunity for a person, while still of sound mind, to appoint a trusted friend, relative or carer as a proxy to decide on matters of medical treatment should the person making the will become incapacitated. The living will might work well in the case of a major accident resulting in a person ending up in a persistent vegetative state, when questions of maintaining the shell of life have to be taken. It does not seem to get over the problems involved in the gradual decline of a person through terminal illness, however, except possibly at the very end when that person has lapsed into the final coma – but when voluntary euthanasia presumably is no longer applicable as the patient is, by then, no longer in pain or distress.

If it is illegal to aid a person in committing suicide, as it is in Britain under the 1961 Suicide Act, how can one be sure that a person depressed and frustrated by illness is not seeking voluntary euthanasia as a form of suicide? Suicide is the ultimate human right, it might be argued, except that few people commit suicide as a recourse of first resort. It is not a right they would choose to exercise except in extreme despair. Should not the despair be addressed first? People prefer to be happy and fulfilled and content. Suicide is the option for those who are not and who are looking for a way to escape their human rights and duties, not to fulfil them.

There are around 6,000 suicides a year in Britain. There are now websites giving advice on how potential suicides can kill themselves which, according to one estimate, were visited 6 million times in 1998. Many of those contacting the sites were under thirty-five and male. One website is run by an American 'church of euthanasia', which also published a magazine called *Snuff It* that advocated suicide, abortion and cannibalism. The church of euthanasia might be seen to be at the extreme, or loopy, end of the spectrum, but it meets a need, feeds fantasies and might eventually contribute to tragedy. It helps create a climate for the acceptance of cheap death. Death is cheapened when it is both on demand and stripped of its spiritual dimension. Those who believe they have nothing in this life and believe they can consign themselves to oblivion treat death as cheap because they regard life as worthless.

By way of a complete contrast there are those, again centred in the USA, but not exclusive to it, who share in the view that physical life on earth is the only kind of life, but who come to a very different set of conclusions from the church of euthanasia. They are the people who say that as there is nothing beyond, then eternal life must be pursued in the physical form. Eternal Flame is a group of like-minded individuals who, like those who have chosen to have themselves frozen at the point of death, chase the butterfly of immortality. They call themselves the Immortals and they say that death is no more than a bad habit. Eternal Flame was founded almost forty years ago in the USA by a former Christian minister, Chuck Paul Brown. It is one of several organizations claiming to have the secret of eternal life and, in most cases, members pay to have lessons in achieving that end. 'Being immortal is terribly exciting, a wonderful adventure,' one Immortal was quoted as saying. He added, 'Being immortal is like living in a concept and the crux of the concept is that we create everything, including the time we choose to die. People tend to die when their death urge exceeds their life urge.'[6]

Immortals describe death as being about separation. Being an Eternal Flame member, they say, is about living together. One member and his wife ran workshops in 'healing sex', claiming that they could help participants release death from their sexual organs. Eternal Flame has been accused of taking advantage of people's fear of death. At its community in Arizona it was observed in 1990 that its 200 or so members were predominantly elderly. From time to time a member died, but, other members said, only because they had been unable to make the changes in their cultural programming in time. Illnesses, they say, are created by people and if that is the case they can also reverse the disease process.

The organization is presumably expressing a view that is no more than the logical extension of modern secular medicine. Death is to be held at bay and if it wins, then that is a failure of medicine rather than an inevitable natural occurrence.

While physical immortality is a hope and dream to Eternal Flame members and others of like mind, to many people it sounds like a form of damnation. There are several folk tales which express the archetypal fear of eternal physical life. There is one legend told of the wandering Jew who has lived for many centuries roaming Europe, taking on new identities as he goes. He can never settle, never make new friends, for fear of losing contact with them through death, and has an eternal future ahead of him of earthly tribulation and disappointment. In some versions of the story he is condemned to his fate for having witnessed the crucifixion of Jesus and done nothing to prevent it.

It is no wonder, then, that almost all religions point to a future of promise in another dimension and one in which the ego is diffused with the greater good and time ceases to have any meaning. To the Jains, for example, this is the description of the final pure state of Moksa, or Siddha, when the person experiences a complete detachment from the affairs of the universe and the soul abides in a state of eternal calm, bliss and total knowledge. Muslims have the promise of a garden of paradise and flowing rivers where the righteous, those who hold their Lord in awe, will dwell forever. God will be well pleased with them and they with him. And what almost all faiths have in common is the notion of surrender. In Christianity it takes the form of giving oneself up to God. It is the surrender at the point of death which provides the transition to eternal spiritual life. And the dying process can itself be a form of surrender.

But is the person who dies at their own hand, or with their own connivance, surrendering to death? Not if surrender means that the ego gives itself over entirely to its future in trust. Determining one's own death is the opposite of that. It is the last defiant act of will to ensure that at the moment of physical death the ego has the final say. Similarly the pursuit of earthly immortality is a deliberate attempt to avoid surrender of self.

Acceptance of the inevitability of death, however, is not the same as surrender, says Kathleen Dowling Singh. Acceptance is the cessation of outward struggle:

> Surrender is of an entirely different order. Surrender is a stance
> of the whole being in which resistance, at any level, ceases as one

willingly becomes active in what is. Surrender is not so much agreeing to, but agreeing with. With surrender, we cease being a victim of life. Gradually… every eventuality becomes another opportunity for awakening. Surrender is infinitely deeper and more thorough, and therefore infinitely more transforming, than acceptance.[7]

Acceptance could be said to relate to physical death while surrender relates to the growing awareness of the possibilities of spiritual life and is a form of preparation for the journey forward to the life hereafter.

In the case of sudden death what happens to the process of surrender? Does it occur on the other side of death when it is realized that death has happened? Or is the whole process of surrender shortened to fit the time available? In modern language, is the dying soul shot forward along a very fast learning curve? Who knows? Can the spirit remain earthbound for a while while matters are resolved? If time loses its meaning at the point of death, then the process of surrender needs no time dimension.

When people die suddenly, and are not consigned to oblivion, are they aware that they are dead? Or are they like the dinner-party guests in the Monty Python sketch who are visited by the grim reaper? They offer him a drink and invite them to join them, not realizing that they have just been killed by a dodgy salmon mousse and that Mr Death, as they call him, has come to take them away to the next world.

And what would happen in the extreme case of simultaneous projection of the human race into the unknown, as is prophesied by so many religions – the moment when the world ends, when God returns, of the final judgement?

CHAPTER NINE

We Will All Go Together, When We Go

'We will all go together, when we go,' is a line from an upbeat song of black humour composed by the American singer-songwriter Tom Lehrer. The theme of the song is nuclear holocaust and it was written during the Cold War when the fear of imminent nuclear destruction was very real. In his sick idiosyncratic manner Lehrer put voice to the worries of millions of people. 'We will all fry together, when we fry,' is another line from the same song which includes the couplet, 'No one will have the endurance, to collect on his insurance... Lloyds of London will be loaded when we go.'

The apocalypse scenario of the 1950s and 60s was centred on the possibility of mutual nuclear annihilation. When President John F. Kennedy and the Soviet leader President Kruschev played their game of international end-time poker over the issue of Russian missiles being sent to Cuba in 1962, many people thought they were on the brink of extinction. A deep sense of fear was experienced across the globe. The military tactics of the time were described by the highly appropriate acronym MAD – Mutually Assured Destruction. Peace was maintained as long as both sides in the Cold War, the East and the West, had a balance of nuclear power and the ability to be able to destroy the other side if subjected to a nuclear attack. The awesome power of the nuclear arsenal was paraded for each side to see. Weapons were tested on a regular basis and after each explosion one superpower would boast that it had out-megatonned the other. It became increasingly dangerous as others joined in and it ceased to be a game restricted to the two sides. France and Britain maintained their 'historic' right to hold their weapons independently. China joined the club as have India, Pakistan and Israel.

Some Christians, in a seemingly perverse interpretation of scripture, appeared to almost welcome the possible nuclear exchange. It would be the final battle, they argued. Armageddon, as described in the Bible, could well be a forecast of nuclear war:

> Then the seventh angel poured his bowl on the air; and out of the sanctuary came a loud voice from the throne, which said, 'It is over!' And there followed flashes of lightning and peals of thunder, and a violent earthquake, like none before it in human history, so violent it was. The great city was split in three; the cities of the world fell in ruin... Every island vanished; there was not a mountain to be seen. Huge hailstones, weighing perhaps a hundredweight, fell on men from the sky.[1]

Islam also teaches that the end of the world will come as a day of immense destruction. The belief is that everything in the world, humans and every living creature, will die. The sun and the moon will lose their gravity and collide. The mountains, it is said, will fly like carding wool. And on that day will come the great resurrection: God will create a new earth and all people who have ever lived will be brought back to life. It will be a day of judgement as every individual will be asked by God to account for their lives. The good will be rewarded and the bad will be punished.[2]

Today, following the end of the Cold War, the fear of nuclear war triggered by the superpowers has receded. Remaining is the threat posed by maverick nation states which threaten to develop nuclear technology, by terrorist groups and by the possibility of accident should some of the weapons in the old Soviet arsenal, which are in an increasingly unstable condition, accidentally detonate. Some nuclear analysts argue that the threat from nuclear weapons is every bit as great as it ever was, but in the public mind the intense sense of fear experienced thirty and forty years ago, when the world lived under the threat of the mushroom cloud, has subsided.

The nuclear fear has been replaced by others which surfaced at the time of the change from the second to the third millennium. The above passage from Revelation is now being cited as a prophetic message of cosmic destruction. Will a comet collide with the world and bring the end of life in its wake? Will a huge meteorite crash into the earth? It is estimated that as many as 500 meteorites hit the earth every year, although most are burned up in the atmosphere prior to landing and create the spectacle of shooting stars. Early in the twentieth century a meteorite narrowly missed crashing onto St Petersburg, landing instead with great force on an uninhabited part of Siberia. In 1998 an asteroid one mile in diameter is calculated to have missed the earth by six hours, and there are 1,000 similar objects known to be orbiting the sun which could potentially collide with earth. Astronomers estimate that the orbits of only 5 per cent of the major meteorites and comets of the solar system are known and any one of the remaining 95 per cent could, in theory, hit the earth. At least one asteroid of notable size, in this case nine miles in diameter, is known to have struck the earth, but this was 65 million years ago.

There are several current cosmic doomsday theories, and as well as meteorite or comet collision there is the fear that the sun will explode, the fear of the solar system being sucked into a wandering black hole and the worry that the earth's axis will wobble causing a change in orbit around the sun, earthquakes and terrestrial instability.

Throughout history collective anxieties have developed which agitate large groups of people, if not entire populations. It could be argued that fears of a great collective end have been one of the driving forces of history. The early Christians were utterly convinced that the apocalyptic second coming of Christ was imminent. Their dedication and courage enabled the message of Jesus to survive persecution and grow into the force it is today.

Do some people thrive on apocalyptic fear? Is there perhaps a basic human need for people to explore the notion that death need not be an individual experience, but could be a collective one imbued with meaning? Sometimes, sadly, these prophecies of the end become self-fulfilling and as already mentioned cult members commit suicide en masse to hasten their departure from the earth. In 1997, thirty-nine members of the Heaven's Gate cult killed themselves, believing that they were about to be taken in spirit to an approaching comet. They were found neatly lying on bunk beds, dressed in black and covered with purple shrouds.

There are certainly many Christians today who firmly believe that the end-time is upon us. They understand the term to mean that sequence of events prophesied in the Bible when Christ will return in majesty. One group has even placed a television camera on the Mount of Olives in Jerusalem, watching over the Golden Gate through which Christ will, it is said, enter the holy city. The picture from the camera is transmitted twenty-four hours a day across the world on the internet. Many preachers monitor international news bulletins for indications that end-time prophecies are about to be fulfilled. One British evangelist who frequently visits Russia and the old Soviet states recently identified the Russian politician Eugene Primakov as a possible candidate for the role of Antichrist.[3]

There is mounting evidence for the growth of apocalyptic beliefs, wrote Damian Thompson: 'Every year millions of people in the Third World are converting to fundamentalist Christianity which teaches that the second coming is at hand. In traditionalist Catholic circles from

Argentina to Japan, there is mounting excitement over worldwide apparitions of the Virgin Mary which foretell the "collapse of evil" and the triumph of the papacy.[4]

There are signs, too, that the concerns of environmental scientists concerning global warming and pollution are gaining popular acceptance. In the summer of 1999 there was great concern because the seer Nostradamus had predicted catastrophe for that time, although when a great terror failed to materialize from the skies in July and August, his credibility was somewhat dented.

When 1999 got underway it seemed, according to many prophets of doom, that it was to be a special year of major disaster. Paris was to be destroyed on 11 August as the Russian space station crash-landed on the French capital. The entire world was due to end in July, or September or November, depending on who was making the prediction. Even at the very highest levels in government in the USA apocalyptic fears were rife. One former senator, now a member of the Clinton administration, Tim Wirth, is convinced that the world is becoming rapidly unstable as a result of population increase. Vice-president Al Gore's favoured end-of-the-world scenario involves the alarming rate at which the human population is consuming the planet's natural resources. President Clinton himself is said to have been much influenced by forecasts of the coming anarchy due to the pressures from diminishing resources and a polluted planet failing to satisfy the demands of an increasing urban population.

As 1999 came to an end there were millions around the world who were convinced that the economic and technological foundations of the Western world would collapse due to the 'millennium bug' in the world's computer systems. In Britain emergency planners were told to report for duty on the night of 31 December in preparation for airliners falling out of the skies and massive power failures. The Bank of England printed double the amount of paper currency to cater for the growing fear that the banking system would be devastated by the failure of the information network to recognize the four digits of the year 2000.

Doomsday scenarios, whether ancient or modern, appear much the same. They are collections of ideas which feed and feed off popular anxiety. At their most intense they involve the idea that human life as we know it will come to an end in an instant, in the twinkling of an eye.

Some say it will be a time when God's power will be seen and felt by everyone. There will no longer be a need for faith; everyone will know that God exists as he will show himself to all. This is a belief shared by several religions. It will be the day of resurrection, it is said, when all those who have died sometime in the past will rise again. That is why it is important in some faiths for a body to be buried intact and not cremated or have parts removed before burial. If each person is destined to rise again then presumably the experience of dying will be like that of dreamless sleep. Time will pass in an instant and on waking the soul will rise to a new life in God's kingdom.

Christians and others who believe that the world was created by God for a purpose also accept that one day the world will come to an end at a time and in a way decided by God and for a purpose of his choosing. People who believe that the world evolved by chance over millions of years tend to believe that the world will end through some chance mishap, and that neither the original development of sentient, intelligent and conscious life, nor its demise, will have been or will be for any discernible reason.

Both religious believers and materialists accept that the end will one day come and that the matter existing in the universe will be recycled – atoms to atoms, dust to dust. Where they differ is that the former believe we shall all survive in spirit and the latter believe that we shall be consigned to nothingness.

CHAPTER TEN

Graves and Grieving

In many parts of the world, the cemetery is a meeting place. Every weekend families arrive to place new flowers on family graves and take the opportunity to catch up with the gossip as old friends arrive to tend the graves of their families. Because the graves are visited so regularly, they become important objects in themselves. In some parts of Europe, it is the tradition for a photograph of the dead parent or grandparent to be incorporated into the design. Inscriptions give more than just name and dates, they give a brief history of a life celebrated. By looking at the grave and pondering the evidence the visitor can get a real feeling for the character being celebrated.

British cemeteries are rather bleak and empty places, and especially so if they are modern or consist largely of small closely ranked tablets marking the spot where ashes have been buried. Only in the older churchyards and on memorials inside historic church buildings are there signs of a more lively way of remembering the dead, of which these are examples:

> Here snug in grave my wife doth lie
> Now she's at rest, and so am I.

Beneath this stone is laid
A noisy antiquated maid,
Who from her cradle talked till death
And ne'er before was out of breath.

My time was come! My days were spent!
I was called – and away I went!!!

Today black humour and originality are outlawed by ecclesiastical regulations. In one notorious case a church official told a grieving family it was forbidden to use the familiar word 'Dad' on a tombstone as it was out of keeping with the tone of the graveyard. The official argument goes that headstones have to meet a minimum standard of good taste. But taste is very subjective and also ephemeral. What is good taste to one generation is naff to the next.

But it is still possible for headstones to be individually commissioned from artists who specialize in producing dignified yet original memorials. When a quality headstone, produced with imagination and the highest craftsmanship, is seen in a graveyard it immediately stands out. In the burial ground of the church dedicated to St Rumwold on the edge of Romney Marsh in Kent there is an exquisitely carved wooden memorial which catches the eye straight away. It is modern, but does not appear out of place among the ancient stones.

The artist Harriet Frazer became interested in the subject of headstones when she was searching for a suitable memorial for her stepdaughter Sophie, who had committed suicide as a young woman in her twenties: 'When she died, I discovered that the deeply bereaved are in a new land. I had never heard of monumental masons. I looked one up in the *Yellow Pages*, and when I got there, there were carpets on the floor and gladioli in a vase and a woman behind a desk. I tried to explain what Soph was like and she said, "Ah, you'll be wanting E2218 in our catalogue."'[1] If the commercialism and marketing of the monumental mason's products was offputting enough, the church bureaucracy was worse. Norwich diocese decreed that a poem written by Sophie would not be permissible. 'We live in an age of anything goes. But in the churchyard so-called good taste often denies humanity or feeling.'[2]

Often, the same monitoring of taste extends to the funeral service, and one survey revealed a telling account from a daughter of her father's funeral. The clergyman taking the service banned 'Dad's favourite music, so we had organ music which Dad would have hated'.[3] While many clergy exercise a great deal of pastoral care in arranging the right funeral for the right occasion, there are others whose own views and prejudices weigh more heavily than the wishes of the family.

A correspondent to *The Church Times* in autumn 1998 wrote of difficulties encountered in trying to arrange a funeral in one Anglican church. The incumbent was asked specifically to use the form of service found in The Book of Common Prayer. Three times the correspondent checked that this would be the case. 'When it came to the day, we had the opening sentences all right, but once we were inside the church the Prayer Book service was ditched in favour of a short address and a "eulogy" of the deceased; no psalm, no scripture reading, no BCP prayers.'[4]

While an insensitive funeral can be distressing, a dull and inappropriate headstone has the more long-lasting effect. Harriet Frazer now offers her services as an artist to bereaved families and helps them get the ideas they feel most appropriate designed and accepted. But it is not always easy. There was the case of the woman known by everyone as Poppy, but whose pet name was not allowed to be used on her grave: 'She was born when the poppies were out. In the end she was buried with a name she was never known by. Once people are squashed into rules, they can't express themselves. If you see "Our Dear Nan" on a tombstone, it gives you a clear picture of this nice, warm woman.'[5]

Gravestones and memorials exist for the benefit of those who are left behind after a death. What is said on them gives us no indication as to what happens to the deceased after death. They are, however, a very good indicator as to what a society believes happens after death and how a culture wishes to present death to its people.

The way the words are presented on a stone is also important. Bland lettering can be very uninspiring. When text is carved in a glorious script or designed to blend in with the natural shape of the stone it can become a work of beauty as well as a means of conveying information. There is a collective of artists calling itself Memorials by Artists which offers a range of choices and styles aiming to create in every gravestone a work of art. In one work by the artist David Holgate the letters follow the natural contours of the slate on which they are carved. The slate resembles a river bed and the words read, 'For life and death are one, even as the river and sea are one.'

Reviewing an exhibition of the collective's work at Blickling Hall in Norfolk, Richard Davey wrote,

> Symbols have always had an important part to play in memorials. In the eighteenth and nineteenth centuries skulls and cherubs reminded the mourner of both heaven and earth; and in many of these modern memorials we find the use of visual symbols. Some provide a narrative illustration for the text, while others portray something about the individual. A beautiful peacock fans its wings in Peter Forster's *Headstone with Peacock*; while two fish, one of which is half-eaten and the other whole, humorously illustrate Mark Evans's text, 'Nothing Lasts, Nothing is Lost'.[6]

The normal rigid control of the design of headstones in Britain suggests that officialdom wishes to retain death as a matter for the professionals only. As far as possible death is sanitized and this suits those running a well-ordered society. Too much concentration on death and too much openly expressed grief might be detrimental to the smooth running of the system. Think of the alarm among many establishment figures when, following the death of Princess Diana, there were outbursts of grief which were unexpected and entirely untypical of the British people. Many people found that through mourning Diana they could mourn for those they had loved and lost whose deaths had never been fully acknowledged in grief.

There is perhaps a fear that uncontrolled grief can turn to anger and from that anger awkward questions might emerge. For instance, suppose a child was killed by a juggernaut lorry driven along a country lane. There is no way that the grieving relatives would be permitted to display their anger on their child's headstone: 'In memory of John, a child killed by the greed of the road lobby.' Far better something bland and reassuring be put: 'In memory of John, taken to be with God. "Suffer the little children to come unto me."'

A little sugary religion is permissible, but dark, demanding questions are not. Ideally, it would seem, the modern human-remains-disposal industry would like everyone cremated at soulless crematoria where expressions of grief are limited to officially endorsed formulae of words. The impression is given that the industry wants all funerals arranged along well-rehearsed guidelines. Standard packages are offered to which only approved extra options may be added so that the funeral 'product' on offer is convenient to arrange and leads to the maximization of corporate profits.

The funeral industry is the capitalist's ideal. The demand is constant, the customers vulnerable and suggestible with no preconceived ideas on appropriate costs. The average British funeral costs a little under £1,700. This figure is arrived at by adding the average standard charge to the average figure of optional extras purchased. The product lines are easy to control and manage and selling optional extras to relatives is where much of the industry's profit comes from.

The American funeral brand SCI, Service Corporation International, controls a substantial proportion of the British funeral industry. One might think one is going to a local family business, but look carefully and the chances are the SCI brand will be lurking in the background. The UK arm of SCI calls itself the country's premier provider of funeral services. As with any multinational corporation its marketing strategies are based on thorough market research and it carries out client surveys to this end. It publishes a quality-standards manual entitled *Client Experience* to ensure that it gives a consistent service. It could be said to be the McDonald's of the undertaking business: 'It's the ultimate commercialism, the final tastelessness. McDeath is on its way to a funeral parlour near you.'[7]

SCI has had some very bad press in Britain. In one television programme in the *Undercover Britain* series,[8] members of SCI staff were shown behind the scenes at a funeral business, handling and talking about bodies in their care with coarse irreverence. The company has responded with a vigorous defence. It condemned bad practice as identified by the documentary, but made no apology for its modern business methods. Society had changed enormously, it said, and people's needs and expectations were very different from those of the days of the old-fashioned funeral. Jayne Farrin, SCI's British director of corporate affairs, told a conference at the Anglican theological college Westcott House,

> Many of the images of the British way of death derive from the idealized Victorian funeral – horse-drawn carriages, mourners in black, widow's weeds and the central role of the Church of England... These kinds of funerals only ever formed a tiny minority... Many thousands of people were forced into having pauper's funerals. Others hoarded their dead bodies until they could afford a funeral.[9]

She spoke of the great variety of funeral custom around Britain and said that there was no simple stereotypical British funeral. In parts of South Wales and in the Hebrides it is still not done for women to attend funerals. In some parts of Bradford it is the custom to walk around the open coffin in the church before the service. In some parts of Britain the demand is for light-coloured coffins. In other parts dark coffins are generally preferred. In parts of the East End of London no one wants a funeral to start too early in the morning as that was the time when, in the days of the Poor Laws, the paupers' funerals took place.

But despite the surviving differences, the general trend has been away from reliance on the traditional sources of support towards buying in the specialist services of the professionals. The process has been very similar to that experienced in many other walks of life: supermarkets have replaced small-town groceries. Call centres are replacing high-street-bank branches. As Jayne Farrin said,

> Over time, the levels of support for the bereaved family have shifted from neighbour, carpenter and village priest to medical personnel, funeral director and crematorium operative. In reality the individual's direct experience and participation in the funeral and death process has actually decreased… Death is more sanitized, isolating and remote for many of us… Death has been placed in the dark attic room of the contemporary developed world.[10]

In an honest assessment of the market need she and her company were currently meeting, she described the commercial climate in which she worked. For most clients, she said, death remained a taboo subject. The funeral process was shrouded in mystery as most adults probably only had to arrange one or two funerals in a lifetime. As the world becomes more complicated, so death retains its simple harrowing truth. Yet there remains a spark of hope in the belief of a life ever after. A good funeral can waken a latent faith which has become buried over the years people have spent coping with and living in an increasingly secular world.

Cynics would say that in life we are all pawns in the world of the market economy. In life our credit details, purchase preferences and a whole host of intimate details are kept on computer. When we shop with a loyalty card at a supermarket the computer notes every item purchased and shapes the shop's advertising strategy accordingly. Closed-circuit television cameras watch our every move. A shopper in an afternoon is typically watched by 300 different cameras. Our choices are manipulated overtly and covertly. Supermarket shelves are designed to fool us into buying what we have no intention of buying. And so it is in death. Relatives are expected to purchase the funeral options on offer. The death business exists to squeeze the very last drop of cash out of a purchaser's life.

A few people like Harriet Frazer look to do something different. There are some who prefer a true do-it-yourself funeral and shun the public crematorium and plush-carpeted undertaker's chapel of rest. More and more people are being buried in shrouds and having trees planted as headstones. Green funerals might be the minority choice, but they are on the increase. Gilly Adams and Sue Gill, the founders of an arts company called Engineers of the Imagination, are arrangers of funerals with a difference. They believe that every funeral is an opportunity to celebrate a life and they create individualized ceremonies, including woodland burials and seashore rituals, which they call 'dead-good funerals'. They have commissioned brightly painted environmentally friendly coffins made from tough cardboard.

The law is more sympathetic to green funerals than it once was. A Scottish farmer made legal history in 1999 when he won the right to be buried on his own land without planning permission. He hoped his last resting place would be a wildflower meadow near his home on Deeside. Ian Alcock had prepared for the event by buying body bags for himself and his wife and building a crude wooden coffin, which he kept in his turnip store. He fixed rope handles on it and sprayed RIP on the side with sheep dye. He was able to satisfy the planning authorities, on appeal, that digging a small number of graves did not constitute an engineering operation as proscribed in planning law. 'I really don't care tuppence what happens to me when I snuff it,' Mr Alcock said after his court victory, 'but I want as simple a funeral as possible. And let's face it, this is getting about as simple as you can get.' After his death, Mr Alcock said the field would not become a designated burial ground, but continue, he hoped, to be used for grazing sheep.[11]

By and large it is only the few eccentrics who make such plans.

Most people have little choice of what kind of funeral to arrange, and at the time of a death they are not in the right state of mind and have little time to explore imaginative options. Decisions have to be taken quickly. Alternative funerals have to be planned well in advance. There is, however, an increasing number of organizations offering funerals with a difference whose contact telephone numbers are often available through local libraries and on the internet.

Planning a funeral often has therapeutic value, especially if a dying person is in the right frame of mind and has the strength to do so. It is a way of integrating this world with the next, whatever form that might take. The commercial funeral does not appear to serve this purpose. It has an empty finality to it and is not a way of bridging this world with the next. At the crematorium, when the curtains close on the coffin, it is the symbol of the end.

Yet funeral rites evolve to be appropriate to the age and society to which they apply and presumably a McDeath fast-funeral service, branded and marketed, is appropriate to people living in the modern market economy where most purchases they make are determined by the marketing and branding of goods.

If funerals in the future are to become more and more commercial products, a tension will arise between the new sellers of funerals and those institutions like the churches which traditionally played a key role. At present, of the 600,000 funerals conducted in England every year, over 400,000 are still conducted by a minister of the established church. The November 1998 General Synod of the Church of England debated the subject and fears were expressed that the church was increasingly being squeezed out of its role as crematoria and small firms of funeral directors were taken over by the likes of SCI.

One particular area of tension is likely to concern the funeral ombudsman, an industry-based arbitration service which relatives may contact and complain to should funeral arrangements fall short of the standard paid for. Will Anglican clergy fall within the remit of the ombudsman? Following the General Synod debate, the holder of the post, Professor Geoffrey Woodruffe, said that the church's willingness to be involved would be 'good news' for consumers.[12]

Traditional funeral rites in many cultures consist of two parts. What is often missing from the commercial product is the second part. The first part of a funeral deals with the past life, personality and social position of the individual. Relatives, friends and work colleagues assemble to pay their respects to someone who had a role to play in their lives. The second part comes later when it is acknowledged that the person who has died has gone on to something else. If the first part is the crematorium service, then the second part is the scattering of the ashes. Often this is done with little ceremony at the crematorium, or by a small group of relatives in a short private ceremony.

A new funeral liturgy drafted by the Church of England in March 1999 provides a set of words to be used at a burial or disposal of ashes. The suggested greeting to be used by the minister encapsulates the notion of a two-part funeral rite: 'Though we are dust and ashes, God has prepared for those who love him a heavenly dwelling place. At his/her funeral we commended *N* into the hands of Almighty God. As we prepare to commit the remains of *N* to the earth we entrust ourselves all who love God to his loving care.'[13]

The second part of the service acknowledges that the person who has died and those who have survived have acquired a new status. For instance, a wife becomes a widow and the deceased ceases to be the head of the household, or the provider, and becomes a soul protected by the hands of God.

Before the funeral the corpse exists as a social and biological entity. Many funeral directors embalm the body if a funeral is to be deferred. One purpose of a funeral is to allow a transition to take place. The rite changes the status of the body from being the shell of a once-living member of the society to being the remains of a departed member of the society. The second part of the rite in particular relocates the dead in the other world, heaven or the place of the ancestors. This relocation has a practical psychological purpose. It stops those who survive dwelling on the realities of decay. Grandfather may in truth be decomposing, but in imagination he is located in a far more pleasant place. If the decaying realities of death possessed our minds, who would have the courage to live?

The contemporary sociologist Zygmunt Bauman sees death as such a profound problem that it may swamp human beings and their will to live. Bauman suggests that the institutions of society, including the churches, actively hide the reality of death. They try to give the impression that death is under control, not least through religious ritual. 'While the reality of death cannot be totally eliminated,' writes Douglas Davies in a review of Bauman's work, 'death rites do their best to keep its impact to a minimum. Bauman's view is strongly of the opinion that ordinary social life might well be seriously damaged if the fact of death was allowed a free hand to strike at people.'[14]

The pessimistic view of Bauman can be challenged from a historic perspective. The fact from some of the most tragic episodes in human history, including even the Nazi holocaust, is that human beings preserve a remarkable degree of hope and dignity when death is all around.

The rituals of the funeral perhaps serve another purpose. Are they the faint echo of the transcendence promised to all those who die in faith? As will be explored later, what happens after death might be, for the departed soul, the beginning of an experience beyond our capacity to even imagine. For those who grieve, who wish to say their farewells to someone they will not see on this earth again, whose love and loyalty they will not feel again, there is sorrow. But the funeral rite exists to say to them, Do not think solely of your loss as you bid farewell, but project forward in your mind to the glory and safety of the next world. 'In your great mercy gather him/her into your arms,' beseeches the new Anglican liturgy, 'and fulfil in him/her the purpose of your love. That rejoicing in the light and refreshment of your presence, he/she may enjoy that life which you have prepared for all those who love you.'[15]

And even if the mourners believe death is the end, the funeral and the permanent memorials may still serve to preserve something of the character or essence of the departed, if only in memories which the living may cherish.

CHAPTER ELEVEN

Public Mourning

There are moments in history when the death of a single public figure becomes a defining moment. Similarly there are times of collective tragedy, war, famine or accident that etch themselves on the collective conscience in a powerful way.

These are times when societies have the opportunity to take stock. When Diana, Princess of Wales, died in 1997 millions of people around the world were touched by the significance of the event. It symbolized so much. A beautiful woman, who had every material benefit this world could offer, was being driven at high speed through the streets of Europe's city of romance with her lover when – suddenly it was over. But for the intervention of her former husband, the authorities might have followed the procedures normally taken in such circumstances and her corpse would have been taken to a public mortuary.

As the eight days of mourning that followed her death produced scenes never before witnessed in London, many people felt that through mourning the princess they had never known they were enabled to grieve for those they had lost for whom they had not wept tears. The funeral service itself drew on popular iconography and

Christian literature to put into words what millions of people felt. The anthem by John Tavener which the choir sang in Westminster Abbey drew on almost every emotive image:

> Alleluia. May flights of angels sing thee to thy rest.
> Remember me O Lord, when you come into your
>   kingdom.
> Give rest O Lord to your handmaid, who has fallen
>   asleep.
> The choir of saints have found the well-spring of life,
>   and door of paradise.
> Life: a shadow and a dream.
> Weeping at the grave creates the song:
> Alleluia. Come, enjoy rewards and crowns I have
>   prepared for you.[1]

One of the functions of a funeral is for the mourners to take away with them an encapsulated version of the person's reputation. The funeral oration or sermon aims to do this. Earl Spencer's address to the Abbey and nation was what was required for the day to freeze dry the image of his sister he wanted posterity to recall.

Diana was in her life, and remains after death, a figure of legend. She was the archetypal Cinderella, virgin bride, wronged wife, comforter, icon and sacrifice.

The legend of Diana which already existed, and which was threatened by her affair with Dodi Fayed, was thus preserved for all time in death, never to tarnish.

Everyone who experienced the death of Diana, in whatever way, however intimately or distanced from events, came face to face, through her death, with their own mortality, just as we do in smaller groups when we attend funerals of family or friends. If such a beautiful woman can be called by death in such a sudden manner, then everyone's life can be seen to be equally precarious. Her death raised harsh questions which cannot be answered. Why did God allow it? What is to become of her now? Is she destined, as some Christians stated, for hell? Will the angels take her to an eternal rest? Will she be reincarnated, if not in a new life, at least through the deeds and achievements of her children, especially the first-born?

And if it is true that some prophesied her death, was Diana's death predestined, known by a God who did nothing to divert it? Through contemplating such questions, everyone has the opportunity to review their own life. Is it in that that a purpose to a prematurely shortened life can be found?

But we cannot truly grieve for a stranger, wrote Jeremy Seabrook:

> There is surely another element in the sentiments released by her death. In part, we are weeping for ourselves. There is a feeling of possibilities foreclosed, of options cancelled, of futures no longer to be contemplated. We are weeping for our own helplessness in the world. Perhaps there is a sense of the unalterability of things in a social and economic order which is now no longer susceptible to change, no longer open for negotiation.[2]

When President John F. Kennedy died in 1963, people mourned for lost hope. When thousands lined the streets of London to watch the funeral of Sir Winston Churchill in 1965, they were marking the end of an era. Public grief occurs when an individual dies who seems in their life to have encapsulated a particular vision or ideal which dies with them. And in the act of remembrance people are enabled to come together to share a transcendent moment.

Where the soulless crematorium fails, the public funeral succeeds enormously. Art, music, atmosphere and prayer can all be drawn together in such a way that they strike the chords of the emotions irresistibly. This blow to the emotions releases the pain pent up inside, perhaps left over many years from unredeemed sorrow and unresolved guilt.

Many people remain shut off from their realization of God by poverty, despair, sickness, material wealth or privilege, and yet it is possible for those defences to be breached. This can be through the example of a person, through poetry, through music, through the gospel, through grief or through the tapping of an archetypal myth held deep in the shared experience of humankind.

In certain rare, rare moments in human history, millions of people appear to have been touched by God simultaneously. And however briefly or however superficially this might be for some, when it happens collectively, it is an awesome thing. It happened at the most intense moment of Diana's funeral when poetry, grief, music, the flowers on the coffin, the gathering of people at a sacred place, silence and the sound of a muffled peal of bells all combined to produce the effect. It happened, too, when President John F. Kennedy was buried. Reports from the nineteenth century suggest that it happened when Nelson was buried in state: the naval ratings and the ordinary people of the streets claimed the great admiral as their hero.

In the television age, the death of a familiar television personality is an opportunity for the wider public to claim that person as their own. In 1999 two British television presenters died, one suddenly by gunfire and the other after a long battle against cancer.

The deaths of Jill Dando and Helen Rollason were very different, but the public response was not dissimilar. Both had been women whose appeal to viewers was as the plausible neighbour. They were the 'girl-next-door' types with whom viewers readily identified. As television provides entertainment in the home, such ordinary people with just that little bit extra by way of bounce and appeal, become great favourites.

The world of the television industry is élitist. The commissioning editors engage with their audiences at arms' length through market research and focus groups. As many aspiring young graduates of media studies courses discover, getting a job in the media, becoming one of the élite, is difficult. The competition for places in the industry is intense. For all its intimacy at the point of delivery television is a remote medium. The death of a personality breaks down that remoteness.

This was especially so in the case of Helen Rollason, who died in a way with which viewers could easily identify, the circumstances of her death allowing the public to take part vicariously. At the time of her death her aspirations had changed from being those of a high-profile sports presenter to those of any mother faced with her fatal diagnosis. Helen hoped to stay alive until her daughter, sixteen-year-old Nikki, had received her exam results. Helen's concerns in her last days were not for herself, but for her daughter and her future welfare.

People who had themselves lost a mother at a crucial stage in life felt they could empathize with the events of Helen's final illness. For some, Helen's death brought out difficult memories which they could attempt to resolve through the death of someone they never knew, but with whose image and reputation they felt comfortable.

Helen's death prompted Alyce Faye Cleese to recall the death of her own mother from cancer:

> I was a teenager at the time and although I was told she was going to die... I somehow psyched myself up and denied it. I think she had tried to hold on until I had started at university. I came back for her funeral but I think I must have shut down quite dramatically. It was not until the Mother's Day around six months later that I really grieved. I was reading the Sunday paper and opened it to see a big advertisement asking, 'Have you remembered your mother?'[3]

The grief, however, was not resolved for many years and she did not dream about her mother until she herself was married: 'The dream made me realize how angry I had been and how much I missed her, but it was a positive dream.'[4]

Those who do not resolve their grief on their own, or resolve it with the help of a caring and sympathetic partner, may find that a public death acts as a catalyst to their discovery of a way forward. The death of Diana, and the period of bereavement which followed, served that purpose, as newspaper and television reporters discovered as they mingled with the crowds in London. Many individuals admitted to grieving more openly for Diana, whom they had never met, than for a parent or family member, whom they had known intimately. It was as if the collective expression of sorrow was enabling them to express other emotions which had lain suppressed for many years. People openly confessed that they had not shed a single tear for a dead father or mother and yet felt released to weep unashamedly for someone they had only known through the press and television.

Combined with the grief there was guilt. The two often go hand in hand. Family members rehearse over and over in their minds what they might have done: 'If only I had done this... mother might still be alive. If only I had visited her just once more... but now she is dead and I will never be able to say to her that I love her...' There is a whole host of pointless and sometimes damaging self-recriminations which can be imagined.

Teenagers who lose a parent have a special angst. They are at the stage when their feelings towards their parents are ambivalent. They want to be released from their grip, to gain their independence and when a parent dies, it feels as if their wish has come true. They can become eaten with the guilt of that realization.

The death of a parent can also produce feelings of anger which take a long time to surface, as Alyce Faye Cleese described: 'I was very lonely when she died. I was quite angry with her as well. I really needed her... I did not want her to leave.'

When Diana died there were public expressions of contrition. They took the form of editors expressing their regret and readers being effusive in their expressions of personal guilt. 'I hope I am not alone in feeling both outrage and shame at Diana's tragic death,' wrote Dr Richard House in a letter to *The Independent* which was published within twenty-four hours of Diana's death. 'Every single person who has chosen to read the media's intrusive, titillating, voyeuristic, soap-opera-ization of Diana's private life (and there can't have been many who haven't) must bear some responsibility for the appalling circumstances of her death.'[5]

Neal Acherson writing for *The Independent on Sunday* described the outpouring of guilt as 'an orgy of self-reproach'. He attributed it to a pent-up sense of guilt which had been accumulating in England over the years. 'The English', he wrote, deliberately excusing the other nations which make up the United Kingdom, 'have grown to feel bad about themselves.'[6]

As if to illustrate Acherson's point, one of the bouquets at Buckingham Palace, placed there on the day of Diana's death, was accompanied by a particularly uncompromising self-accusation:

> I killed her. I hounded her
> to the death. I followed her
> every movement.
> I gave her no peace. For I bought the papers. I read the
> stories and
> I looked at the photographs.
> They did this for me.
> How can I live with that?

Two years on the self-reproach had turned on a scapegoat. Not the media, as might be supposed, but the House of Windsor and Camilla Parker-Bowles, Prince Charles' unofficial partner. The messages left at Kensington Palace on the second anniversary of Diana's death contained evidence of much hatred. 'Camilla the witch,' said one.

At the time of Princess Diana's death, a significant increase was reported in calls to the Samaritans, the organization which provides support and a listening ear to people contemplating suicide. A spokesman for the Samaritans said that 'in many cases the feelings of grief and anger triggered emotions that may have been hidden for a long time'. Another Samaritan said that Diana's death had caused people to reflect on their own lives. It was thus both a challenging and a cathartic process.

What cannot be gauged is whether the calls to the Samaritans indicated an increase in potential suicides, or simply a need for many people to find someone to whom to unburden. Whichever the case, the result of the process was therapeutic. In the three months following Diana's death some psychiatric clinics were reporting a 50-per-cent reduction in admissions. There was a particular decrease in the numbers of people seeking help for depression, anxiety and stress. The observations of three professionals in the field substantiate this impression.

The cathartic effect was observed by Dianne Trueman, manager of Sutton's Manor Clinic at Stapleford Tawney in Essex. 'When they cried for Diana, many people, particularly men, who often have trouble expressing emotions, found they could also cry for themselves, allowing the release of repressed emotions. We saw a significant decrease in general psychiatric admissions of around 50 per cent. This included private patients and NHS referrals – it is unprecedented.'

Haydn Lunn, manager of the Dove Clinic near Burton-on-Trent, Staffordshire, said, 'There's a significant benefit from a good old cry and the death of Diana gave people the licence to do just that. It allowed people to put their own problems into perspective.'

Angela Martin of Aire Valley Clinic near Keighley, West Yorkshire, said, 'We found that people who would normally keep their emotions bottled up suddenly allowed themselves a complete outpouring of emotion, all tied up in the grief they felt at Diana's death.'

Thus a public death serves many purposes. It is a reminder to all of mortality. In the case of a superstar who dies, it is clear evidence of the truth of one of the core messages of Christianity. It benefits no one to gain the whole world, if they lose their soul. Superstars appear to have achieved everything they could want in life, and yet at the moment of death they are seen as vulnerable and as alone as anyone else. Diana had everything the world could offer and in death lost it all in an instant.

The death of Helen Rollason presented a different message. She was a sports reporter who had radiated good health. Her death from cancer was a reminder that disease can strike even those who are closely identified with bodily excellence. It was a reminder to people not to take anything for granted. What one person has today can be taken away tomorrow for reasons we cannot understand. Yet, as Helen's death also suggested, even in adversity it is possible for courage and goodness to shine through.

Jill Dando's death struck other chords. She was a person whose professional ordinariness was totally unthreatening. What was disturbing about her death was that something so brutal could happen to someone who posed no threat. Her death was neither the result of a random accident, nor of disease, but of an incomprehensible desire, by someone unknown, to see her dead. It was a scary death for people to contemplate, especially as the weeks passed after the event and no killer or motive were found. Questions were asked about her private life. Did something dark lurk behind the golden image? The mystery deepened and those who thought about it began to ask other disturbing questions. Who else, whose appearance we trust, might be hiding a secret?

A public death, to reach through to the public psyche, needs to represent an archetypal fear or widespread concern. From time to time millions become obsessed by the story of a child who might have a fatal disease. The parents travel around the world looking for a cure. The public subscribes to their search and invests its emotions in the quest. When the child dies, there is a shared sense of loss. Other victims of tragedy may be publicly mourned if their deaths represent something wider. The news of the shooting of children at the school in Dunblane touched a very raw public nerve. In an age of anxiety, when children are protected as never before, the one safe haven, the sanctuary away from home, the classroom, had been brutally violated. It was a horrific deed for those involved and a profoundly disquieting one for those who shared the news second-hand.

Both a funeral of a friend and a public death serve the same purpose: they are both a reminder of mortality. Yet it should be emphasized that they are more than that – they are an opportunity. At a private funeral and sharing in a public death an individual has the chance to reflect on what is to come. It is then, during moments of reflection, that the obsessions and concerns of the material can briefly fall away. The rites associated with public grief are especially effective in allowing this to happen. Society allows normal inhibitions to be set aside and through the medium of collective prayer and the hearing of great, evocative music, many thousands of people can have a glimpse of the numinous, and open themselves up to receiving a moment of reassuring transcendence. This point was well appreciated by those who initiated the cenotaph Remembrance Sunday service, and set the pattern for similar services to be held in every town and village to recall those who died in war. While there is now a strong case to be made for changing the service into one which enables people to pledge never to go to war again, for those who lived during the First and Second World Wars, and who mourn friends and relatives, the Remembrancetide services will never lose their poignancy.

CHAPTER TWELVE

The Insight of Children

It has been often said of children that, until school and puberty take over, in their innocence they have a special empathy with matters spiritual. This guileless spirituality can take many forms. The prayers of children can be very revealing. I recall my daughter around the age of five saying she had made up a prayer: 'Thank you horrid God for thistles, brambles and barbed-wire fences.' I told a theologian I knew who spent a long time exploring the prayer's meaning. Also, those who believe in reincarnation see evidence of a spirituality of a different sort, and claim that young children have the most vivid memories of former lives and these memories fade with age.

There are children who have invisible friends. Their parents and teachers might prefer to think of these friends as figments of childish imagination, but there are some who believe otherwise. They say that the friends are spirits of a twin lost in embryo, or that the child is able to see a guardian angel. There is certainly evidence that twins who lose their fellow twin around the time of birth maintain a relationship with that twin throughout life. They talk of the twin as if they had shared a life with him or her, even though, presumably, they have no conscious memory.

So do children who are facing death have any special insights? Can they see beyond the grave? If it is said that at death adults need to relinquish the clutter of life surrounding their own sense of identity in order to find their potential for transcendence, might it be that children, who have a less developed sense of themselves, find they have less clutter to burden them and a more immediate and natural appreciation of matters spiritual?

Children present insights into the realm of the spiritual in another way. Sister Frances, the Anglican nun who founded the hospice for children Helen House, says that no parent ever believes that once their child dies, it is the end:

> Death can be very ugly, but people have buried within them a strength and dignity to meet it; and, given encouragement and loving surroundings, they will do this with what I can only describe as a severe beauty. I believe in the Resurrection, that death is not the end but the beginning, and I have yet to meet a mother or father who believed at the moment of death that their child had ceased to exist.[1]

But what should children be told lies beyond death? The question is bound to be asked when the parent is least prepared, either by a dying child or a healthy child who has come into contact with death. Many children ponder such matters for a long time before posing the question and will rely on the answer.

From an early age it appears that children have learned to differentiate between real death and pretend death. Boys shoot each other with toy guns, they watch 'unsuitably' violent television programmes and zap aliens in computer games. Many girls do as well. Mostly, children are unaffected by real death. But when a pet dies, or an elderly relative, or even a friend at school, real death has to be faced.

Some children when dying are very aware of what is happening to them. Molly, the 14-year-old girl I knew who died and whose funeral I described earlier, shared her thoughts with her close friends, her mother believes. Yet she did not talk about death to her mother directly, perhaps to protect her from her own feelings. So it is not always obvious to adults just how aware children are when approaching death.

Children who are long-term hospital residents mature mentally very rapidly. They may be viewed with sentimental pity by strangers, but they are often tough and resilient beyond their years. They may also appear to demonstrate a remarkable sensitivity to what can be described as a spiritual atmosphere in a sacred place. When my grandson Joshua was eighteen months old he came to our local church for the first time, when there was a flower festival being held. As he walked in, holding his grandmother's hand, he looked around and his face was filled with wonder. He was soaking in the novelty of the sight, but was he also sensing something beyond that?

All humans have the potential for spiritual and religious awareness, believes David Hay, a reader in spiritual education at Nottingham University. However, social pressure often results in that awareness being suppressed. Therefore, he suggests, if we acquire secular behaviour in the course of our upbringing, it would be logical to suppose that the least tainted spirituality is to be found among children.

David Hay, with his colleague Rebecca Hay, made a study of children at two primary schools. One group was aged six and the other ten. 'When we looked closely at what children had to say, it became clear that there was no such thing as a child without spirituality,' they commented.[2]

A few children unselfconsciously expressed themselves in religious terms. Other children conversed in a more detached way, using God-talk as a kind of formula. Still others had a spirituality of struggle, feeling that there was a reality to God, but finding it difficult to make sense of this in a material world. Many children have to make do with fantasy and fairy tales to speak of the deepest things of life. When children talked about their spiritual lives there appeared to be an unusually high level of awareness or perceptiveness, compared with their conversations on other matters. Without exception, all spiritual talk referred to how the children related to reality; to God, other people, themselves or to the material world.

David and Rebecca Hay concluded, 'We need the spiritual insight that is naturally present in all children. It does not have to be taught, only nurtured, protected and reflected upon.'[3]

When a child dies, parents often want to find a way by which they can visualize their child in the next life. The child lives on in memory. There are often photographs to be kept and happy stories to be told and retold by the family. If the child dies at an age when something of the personality of the child has already emerged, it is easier to keep hold of memories. Yet memories are not always enough. Some parents seek the advice of mediums and are given word-pictures of a child in paradise, which for a while they might find comforting. But as suggested earlier, it is unlikely that the medium's message bears any relation to the truth.

Sometimes parents comfort themselves with religious fairy tales. They think of how children, who die in all innocence, become angels in heaven. On occasion some parents might torture themselves with their imaginations. They fear that a child who dies unbaptized is destined for an eternal existence of spiritual limbo. Mothers of aborted babies may have particularly disturbing feelings of guilt.

Opponents of abortion have the right to ask demanding questions about the way abortion is sanctioned. They can argue that to cut short the life of a foetus, however undeveloped, is destroying something of God's creation. However, in fairness to mothers who opt for an abortion, they should also spell out their view, if any, as to what happens spiritually to the aborted child. If the child is already a soul, does that soul go to be with God? If that is the case then the mother who aborts a child has one less thing to feel guilty about. If, conversely, the foetus has no conscious existence and no soul, is its destruction any worse than the destruction of any other part of God's creation – animals, plants or ecosystems?

The process of growing up is a process of discovering oneself. It is the time when the personality takes shape and often problems and anxieties which occur later in adult life can be attributed to difficulties experienced as a young, receptive, sensitive and vulnerable child.

In a paper describing the experience of an 82-year-old woman suffering from panic attacks, Joan Hunter reflected that the attacks could be traced back to an infantile terror of dying: 'Then after she proved able to "remember" this experience... she recalled a communication she had had from her late mother in 1959. This she now construed as a reassurance about dying. After this she spoke increasingly of her more understanding views of others and realistically about her own feelings of approaching death.'[4] The communication with her mother occurred when the woman believed she had heard her dead mother speaking to her, telling her how she was in a state of limbo, unable to enter eternity, because of her anger towards her husband. She felt that after this communication her mother was at peace. Whether this communication was real, or whether it was a figment of the woman's imagination which she created for a purpose, is an open question. I tend to support the latter view.

The dying process is often described as that whereby the ego is released. It involves returning to that state of openness and receptiveness one had been in as a child. If becoming aware of one's spiritual life and, eventually, the attainment of transcendence, starts with the individual shedding the baggage of the earthly world, it might be argued that a child, who has not yet acquired that baggage, is in a state of natural spiritual awareness.

One of the most beautiful underlying messages of the Christmas story is that of the spiritual potential of the newborn child. The story tells of how, in all his vulnerability, the baby Jesus is at one and the same time God. Jesus later endorsed this view of the spirituality of the very young in his call to the little children to come to him. The view that sin has already entered the child from the very start is not, it seems, backed up by the New Testament. The potential for sin may be there, as all people are given free will by God, but right at the start, before any choices have been made, how can it possibly be said that sin has already tainted the child? To hold this view would run counter to the idea of being born again to achieve eternal life. It contradicts those Christians who are obsessed with condemning sins of the flesh and who would say that a child's very conception occurs at a moment of lust.

It may be argued that the younger a child is at the time of death, the more intact will be that spiritual potential. Transcendence into the presence of God will be a short step and not the giant leap adults might have to negotiate. Yet that idea can bring only partial comfort to bereaved families. It is natural to grieve, especially for a child whose life might have been one of great promise. At the hospice for children, Helen House, the care offered is as much for the family as the child. When a child dies he or she is often placed in a small bed in a special room where the parents can sit with the child, bring toys and favourite objects and begin the process of grieving, surrounded by support and love.

Siblings as well as parents need to grieve and ask questions. The death of a brother or sister can be very disturbing. It is not in the nature of the young to consider their own death and yet the death of someone who shared the same home, parents and life turns that remote possibility into a premature reality.

City high-flyer Nicola Horlick nursed her daughter Georgie through a terminal illness and realized afterwards how her other four children had missed her as she spent so much time with the one sick child. 'The other children have hardly seen us,' she reflected after Georgie's death. 'They're still grieving. My youngest is like a limpet. 'Life is unfair. Life is horrible. But someone's got to be the unlucky one. And I feel her spirit is around me, which is comforting. I never thought I'd feel like that.'[5]

Christians can often feel especially angry with God when a child dies, particularly if they had been praying in trust for a recovery from an illness. When Sasha died after eight years of life, her father, Ralph Crathorne, described how he and his family and friends had prayed for her during her five years of illness. When she died he recalled in his funeral address how he was struck by a pain in his heart. But then, he said, the peace of God started to flood through the pain. And following her death 'we had the most wonderful two hours in our room, crying, remembering, trusting, laughing, preparing her body together. Was hers a life tragically cut short? No: we have come to see, even during the hours after her death, that she was given an eight-year life on earth. It was a completed, fulfilled, rounded life.'[6]

A few weeks before she died Sasha asked her mother if she was going to die. And her mother replied, 'All the doctors say so but we do not expect you to. But if you do, you'll go straight to heaven and you'll be in a wonderful place and we'll be there with you in the blink of an eyelid.' Her mother began to cry. 'Come on Mum,' said Sasha, 'Dry your eyes, go and get a tissue and then come back.'[7]

Sasha died in love and faith. Millions of children die every year unloved. They are victims of disease, starvation, war or neglect. Their innocence is confronted and abused by the evil in the world. In the circumstances of their deaths it is hard to think in terms of death coming as a transcendent experience. It is more likely that death is to them a relief, a release from pain and hardship. Their personalities may never have had the opportunity to develop enveloped by love. Many of these neglected children could not expect to have had any view of life other than one which was warped and distorted. When considering death, and the transcendent possibilities which might follow, it is as well not to forget those who do not die in the comfort of their own beds as fulfilled adults. It needs to be asked whether theories about death, which have grown out of the experience of those living in the relative peace and affluence of the Western world, can also apply to those who die in squalor and poverty.

The Mystery of Transcendence

If a person is fortunate enough to have lived a full life, in both years and experience, that person should, as the years passed have grown wiser. Wisdom is often the compensation for growing slower and older as life takes its usual downhill course towards its conclusion. In some cultures age and wisdom are equated and the elderly are specially cherished and revered. (Among families of elephants, by way of an aside, the oldest animal is always the leader, for she has the longest memory and the greatest knowledge of life.)

During our time here on earth we should learn the lessons to be derived from our particular existence. Each experience, whether joyful or sorrowful, will grant us new insights into ourselves and into others with whom we have contact. We might even gather some insights as to the purpose of it all. On the way, through each stage of life, we will, most surely, witness the deaths of others. Some of these deaths will be peaceful, while others will be tragic or violent. We will grieve over many friends and family members whose deaths we do not witness directly.

Some of us might have to physically prepare the dead for burial. Many more of us will have to deal with the practical consequences of death in other less direct ways: executing wills, collecting death certificates and instructing undertakers. As a result all of this experience and responsibility, we will appreciate the first lesson of being close to the reality of physical death: we all, however fit, young or healthy, have a finite hold on life.

By the time our own turn comes to face death we will almost certainly have some gained some understanding of what death is and consequently some of the fear of death might have vanished. Indeed, it is often noticeable with the very old that they look forward to death. 'I think I have had enough,' 'I've had a good innings,' 'I don't want to be a nuisance to everyone any longer,' are phrases frequently used by the elderly, as they look forward to the end.

If the fear of death is fear of the unknown, that fear will surely diminish in part as we become more familiar with the subject. We cannot know what is beyond, but we will have become familiar with the business of seeing people depart on the journey. Understandably, most people feel a little apprehensive as they embark on a journey of any distance. What will happen if connections are missed? Will travelling be enjoyable or stressful? Will the destination be as we hope? Will we know when we arrive?

Awaiting death can be likened to sitting in the departure lounge at an airport waiting for the flight to be called. We may know roughly when the flight will be announced, but not exactly. We sit and wait patiently for an inevitable, but unspecifically timed, event. Sometimes people jump the queue. For one reason or another they are told they are to be fast-tracked onto the plane. Similarly, some people queue-jump life and discover that death is nearer than they thought.

People who are told that they have an untreatable disease and therefore only have a short time to live normally find the news inevitably concentrates the mind on the important things of life. Ambitions and forward planning are put aside. More time is spent with family and friends. People with only a short life ahead, when first adapting to their condition, may dwell on the physical side of death and grow anxious about the process. Will the end come swiftly? Will it be painful or humiliating? We can even find ourselves imagining the state of our body after death – see it in our mind's eye lying inert before the decay sets in.

But more than likely the mind will not dwell on such details. It will become concerned about the future of others. Will our responsibilities towards them have been adequately discharged before we go? Will provision have been made for dependants? Will old feuds have been healed? These anxieties can be addressed by practical action. Wills can be altered, executors nominated, letters written. It is once those tasks have been completed that the mind can turn inwards.

Waiting to go on a journey can also produce a tingle of excitement. It is excitement and hopefulness that spur us on. Death is a journey, perhaps. The soul will be transported to a beyond we cannot and dare not contemplate. Will it be like taking a mystery trip to a faraway and unimaginable land?

Those glimpses of the truth we might have had in life, those moments of transcendence which flashed by yet sustained us and renewed our hope, may hold the key and the promise of what is to come. When time has stopped and pain ceased and the restless demands of the physical world have passed away; when the confusions created as the senses grew more and more feeble and unreliable have resolved themselves in peace, what will be left? Those things which in life existed in us and for us, but which were always obscured by the demands of life and the cravings of the ego.

When 'I' cease to be, in the earthly sense, and all the impediments to knowledge are set aside, perhaps then the light will be clear to see. That light which is, and has always been, in me, but hidden by worldly obsessions. I say light, for that is the best word we have in the English language to describe the inconceivable awareness which might then be ours. John wrote of God, in that glorious opening to his gospel which is the reading in thousands of Christian churches on Christmas Day, 'In him was life; and the life was the light of men. And the light shineth in darkness; and the darkness comprehended it not... That was the true light, which lighteth every man that cometh into the world.'[1]

People who believe that they have experienced death and have returned talk of seeing a light and being drawn towards it and into it. The light, they say, appears to them to be a source of love and as they approach it they have no fear. The experience might be a delusion, or it might be a first glimpse of the reality that is to be.

Elisabeth Kübler-Ross once described an interchange between herself and a patient who was very close to death: 'He experienced himself floating out of his body toward a beckoning light. He said that if he had gone any closer to the light he would not have returned. It was the light of God. God is the light and love these people experience. They are entering his presence. That, for me, is beyond a shadow of a doubt.'[2]

If it is a glimpse of the life to come, it is a very brief glimpse, but enough of a foresight to know that existence beyond the grave will be very different from this one on earth. While it might not be possible to comprehend what that life will be like, one can imagine the excitement of coming face to face with totally different ways of being, thinking and knowing. Not even people with inquisitive minds, with an interest in the many exciting and exotic things this earth has to offer and with the greatest zest for knowledge, can imagine the amazement of what might be to come.

When a baby is born it, too, is suddenly plunged into a world of new experience. It finds much around confusing and fearsome. Only the sure and familiar touch, sight, sound, smell and taste of mother provides a continued link with the world in the womb. As time goes by the child starts to learn that not everything in the new world is frightening. Slowly but surely the child who is loved discovers new sensations.

I recall the wonder on the face of my grandson when, as a baby of a few months, he was shown a flower for the first time. Never having seen anything like it before, he was transfixed by its beauty. As the years go by he will see many flowers, but none, I suggest, will be as delightful and astonishing to him as the first. In touching it, smelling it and attempting to eat it, Joshua had discovered something for which there was no precedent in his life so far.

Similarly, discovering new foods has given him pleasure. His first taste of Yorkshire pudding when he was a little older and had a few teeth was a joy to behold. As he put it in his mouth he was smiling and dribbling and he appeared to be in seventh heaven – such was the novelty and delight of the experience.

But especially I still delight in his expression of excitement and wonder when he hears a new piece of music. Whether he will grow up to be musical I do not know, but at the age of sixteen months, when he came to see his grandparents, he would make a toddling beeline for the shelf of CDs. He would take one, presumably at random, and then ask for it to be played. The moment of waiting must have seemed like an age to him – but then came the music. Were it jazz, classical or even Shetland fiddle music, it never failed to delight him and the sight of him in such enjoyment never failed to warm those watching.

So, life beyond the grave might be one long round of new experiences, of seeing things and feeling emotions one cannot at present even imagine – but without the fear. A person blind from birth has no conception of colour. Maybe, similarly, a person used to life on this earth will have no way of imagining what is meant by the depth of the love of God until the love is experienced in all its glory and intensity. Christians talk in their prayers of the peace of God which passes all understanding. After death perhaps those words will be given their complete meaning.

When a newborn baby enters the new world of opportunity, he or she also comes face to face with the negative side of life from which the womb provided protection. There is physical pain. If the baby is in a premature-baby unit blood tests are taken and tubes inserted. Even today some medical practitioners do things to young children which they would not dream of doing to an adult without anaesthetic. There is cold to contend with and excessive heat. There are the problems of breathing. There may be the jealousy of a sibling to cope with, the resentfulness of a family, even abandonment and desertion in extremis.

The transcendent experience of death does not, presumably, have the same negative side, although the dying process, especially in its early stages, is not easy. There is much to be worked through. The musician Judith Marten-Meynell has said,

> My attitude totally changed once I realized that life and death have no difference. So often the emphasis is just on living, while dying is pushed away for as long as we can keep it at bay. Acceptance frequently only comes when we see death as inevitable. Once I moved into recognizing that life and death are the same thing and that I couldn't grow vegetables in spring if the ground hadn't had its winter, then my perception changed.[3]

Can one put it another way: the darkest part of the night is just before dawn? Transcendence comes out of the travail of the process of dying, just as new life is born into this world following the travail of labour. As many of the famous Christian mystics have discovered, the dark night of the soul comes before the illuminating moment of recognizing God:

> Tomorrow I shall die, and see you face to face; tomorrow your lash on my body shall cease, and I shall be at peace. If now my body is shrouded by clouds of darkness, my soul basks in warm light; if now my eyes are filled with bitter tears, my soul can taste the sweetest honey.[4]

But all of this is speculation. Every thought on the subject must be qualified with such words as 'perhaps' and 'maybe'. Viewed from this side of death the knowledge of what is to come is shrouded by a cloud of unknowing. At the funeral I attended a few years ago of a former dean of Canterbury, Ian White-Thompson, the first reading came not from the scriptures, but from *The Cloud of Unknowing*:

But now you will ask me, 'How am I to think of God himself and what is he?' and I cannot answer you except to say, 'I do not know!' For with this question you have brought me into the same darkness, the same cloud of unknowing where I want you to be! For though we, through the grace of God, can know fully about all other matters, and think about them – yes, even the very works of God himself – yet of God himself can no man think.

Therefore I will leave on one side everything I can think, and choose for my love that thing which I cannot think! Why? Because he may well be loved, but not thought. By love he can be caught and held, but by thinking never. Therefore, though it may be good sometimes to think particularly about God's kindness and worth, and though it may be enlightening too, and a part of contemplation, yet in the work now before us it must be put down and covered with a cloud of forgetting. And you are to step over it resolutely and eagerly with a devout and kindling of love, and try to penetrate that darkness above you. Strike that thick cloud of unknowing with the sharp dart of longing love, and on no account whatever think of giving up.[7]

Could it be, therefore, that our mistake when asking the question, What happens after death? is that we then go on to think too hard about the answer? As with sleep, one cannot find tranquillity, as one tosses and turns in bed, just by anxiously thinking about oblivion and willing it on oneself. It is when the mind is at peace that sleep takes over. 'The Way which can be spoken about is not the Way,' said Lao Tzu, whose philosophy from ancient China has survived several millennia to remain resonant today.

Death is often likened to sleep. The dead rest in peace, they sleep in the Lord, say the headstones. Maybe we would understand both states better by turning that comparison around. Sleep is like death. It is death with a return ticket. In sleep we abandon time. In sleep we transcend the physical burdens of the material world. In sleep we can dream of those we have loved who have died. In sleep, too, we can have nightmares as

our fears, anxieties, insecurities and wrongs catch up with us. 'Sleep...
brother to Death, in silent darkness born,' wrote Samuel Daniel.[5]

And Sir Thomas Browne took the idea further: 'We term sleep a
death and yet it is waking that kills us and destroys those spirits which
are the house of life.'[6] He turned on its head the notion that reality is
when we are awake and dreams are but a shadow of reality. Can that
same reversal of ideas apply to death? Is death reality, and life as we
understand it here on earth but a shadow of that reality?

Moments of transcendence achieved through the discipline of
meditation do not come to those who think too hard. They come when
all is forgotten, when the mind is cleared. And presumably that is what
happens at death: the mind is cleared. At that defining moment all the
earthly impediments to transcendence are removed.

The mourners see the death agonies. They see the stiff corpse. The
undertaker sees his next job. The grave is prepared, the flowers ordered,
the death is registered, the grieving process takes its course. A young
soldier facing the possibility of death in the Second World War wrote,

> If I should pass
> beyond man's thought,
> grieve not...
> For He who plans
> the pattern of the stars,
> who sets each leaf
> on every tree and bush;
> knows of my course...
>
> And if He will my destiny
> be life, that life I seek...
> if death, then death is
> but a gate to truth,
> and more immense
> than all the universe.[8]

A hospice doctor once wrote of a patient that she did not begin to live until she reached the time and the place of her dying – to which another doctor responded, 'Dying is the experience of a lifetime.' And while during life we use the daily prayer taught by Jesus himself – the Lord's prayer – so, at the end of life, there is no better prayer than that given to us by Jesus as he hung on the cross: 'Father, into thy hands I commend my spirit.'[9]

Notes

Introduction

1 T. Harrison, *Living with Kidney Failure*, Oxford: Lion, 1990.
2 C. Saunders, pioneer of the British hospice movement as medical director of St Christopher's Hospice.
3 Psalm 23:4 (KJV).
4 S.B. Nuland, *How We Die*, London: Vintage, 1997.
5 E. Kübler-Ross, *On Death and Dying*, London: Tavistock, 1970.
6 K.D. Singh, *The Grace in Dying*, Dublin: Newleaf, 1998.
7 Nuland, *How We Die*.
8 J.F. Fletcher, *Harpers*, October 1960.
9 Nuland, *How We Die*.
10 Nuland, *How We Die*.

Chapter One

1 V. Ironside, *Arranging the Funeral You Want*, SCI UK.
2 D.J. Davies, *Death, Ritual and Belief*, London: Cassell, 1997.
3 Genesis 22:1–14.
4 A. Ritchie, *Prehistoric Orkney*, London: B.T. Batsford/Historic Scotland, 1995.
5 Ritchie, *Prehistoric Orkney*.
6 G.T. Meaden, *The Stonehenge Solution*, London: Souvenir, 1992.

Chapter Two

1 J. Litten, *The English Way of Death*, London: Robert Hale, 1991.
2 F. Furedi, *Culture of Fear*, London: Cassell, 1997.
3 Furedi, *Culture of Fear*.
4 World Health Organization, 1996.
5 D. Livingstone, *Missionary Travels and Researches in Africa*, 1857.
6 B.O. Smith, in P. Williams and T. Harrison, *McIndoe's Army*, London: Pelham, 1979.
7 I. Lipsiner, in S.B. Nuland, *How We Die*, London: Chatto and Windus, 1994.
8 Nuland, *How We Die*.
9 C. Mims, *When We Die*, London: Robinson, 1998.
10 Singh, *The Grace in Dying*.
11 J. Marten-Meynell, lecturer in music thantology from Missoula, Montana, USA.
12 Singh, *The Grace in Dying*.
13 Nuland, *How We Die*.

14 Singh, *The Grace in Dying*.

15 Singh, *The Grace in Dying*.

16 From an interview of Father O'Leary with the author.

17 R. Gillon, *Withholding and Withdrawing Life-prolonging Medical Treatment*, London: BMJ Books, 1999.

18 Mims, *When We Die*.

19 D. Davies and A. Shaw, *Reusing Old Graves: A Report on Popular British Attitudes*, Crayford: Shaw and Sons, 1995.

20 B. Franklin (1706–90).

CHAPTER THREE

1 F. Bacon (1561–1626).

2 F. Bacon, letter to Lord Burleigh.

3 Psalm 90:4 (KJV).

4 I. Watts (1674–1748), 'O God, Our Help in Ages Past', *The English Hymnal*, Oxford: Oxford University, 1906.

5 T.S. Eliot, 'Little Gidding', *Four Quartets, Collected Poems 1909–62*, London: Faber and Faber.

6 Ecclesiastes 3:1 (NIV).

7 Ecclesiastes 3:2–8 (NEB).

8 Ecclesiastes 3:11, 19–21 (NEB).

9 The Venerable Bede (673–735).

10 Colossians 2:8 (NEB).

11 R.H.J. Steuart, *The Mystical Doctrine of St John of the Cross*, London: Sheed and Ward, 1934.

12 Steuart, *The Mystical Doctrine of St John of the Cross*.

13 S. Hawking, *A Brief History of Time*, London: Bantam, 1988.

14 John 1:1–3 (KJV).

15 A. Quicke, *Tomorrow's Television*, Oxford: Lion, 1976.

16 Quicke, *Tomorrow's Television*.

17 From a report by The Movement for Christian Democracy, 1999.

18 D. Cupitt, 'God Within', *Tradition and Unity*, ed. D. Cohn-Sherbok, London: Bellew, 1991.

19 Davies and Shaw, *Reusing Old Graves*.

20 Davies and Shaw, *Reusing Old Graves*.

21 Davies and Shaw, *Reusing Old Graves*.

22 H.S. Holland (1847–1918).

23 Ironside, *Arranging the Funeral You Want*.

24 C.G. Rossetti, 'Remember'. She was also the author of the much-loved Christmas carol, 'In the Bleak Midwinter'.

25 W.H. Auden, Number 9, 'Twelve Songs', London: Faber and Faber.

26 C.G. Rossetti, 'When I Am Dead'.

27 *Diana, Children's Letters to God*, London: Marshall Pickering, 1997.

28 J. Seabrook, *Resurgence*, January 1998.

29 October 1999, over two years after Diana's death.

CHAPTER FOUR

1 Genesis 28:10–15.

2 C. Gallagher, in R. Vincent, *People Come Back to Me and My Son*, Ireland's Eye, 1992.

3 M. Rawlings, *Beyond Death's Door*, Nashville, Tennessee: Thomas Nelson, 1978.

4 S. Blackmore, *Dying to Live*, London: Grafton, 1993.

5 C. Jung, *Memories, Dreams and Reflections*, London: Collins, 1971.

6 From an interview of Robert Campbell with the author.

7 S. Gordon, 'Blinded by the light', ch. 2, *The Book of Miracles*, Headline, 1996.

8 Gordon, *The Book of Miracles*.

9 D. Lorimer of the International Association for Near-Death Studies, speaking at a conference on death, 1998.

10 Lorimer, speaking at a conference on death.

11 The Dalai Lama, *Kindness, Clarity and Insight*, Snow Lion, 1984.

12 Genesis 2:7.

13 J. Wren-Lewis, in *The New Natural Death Handbook*, Rider, 1997.

14 Gallagher, in Vincent, *People Come Back to Me and My Son*.

15 From an interview with the author.

16 S. Blackmore, quoted in *Fortean Times*, 108.

17 J. Cockell, speaking at the Fortean Times Unconvention, London, 1998.

18 S. Bhavyananda of the Ramakrishna Vedanta Centre.

19 Matthew 11:14.

20 *The Encyclopedia of Mystical and Paranormal Experience*, London: Grange, 1991.

21 M. Bentine, *Doors of the Mind*, London: Granada, 1984.

22 Exodus 22:18 (NEB).

23 Leviticus 19:31 (NEB).

24 Acts 19:19 (NEB).

25 L. Van der Post, *Jung and the Story of Our Time*, London: Hogarth, 1976.

26 From the author's own local research.

27 As reported to the author by a verger at York Minster.

28 From an unsigned letter sent to a religious newspaper.

29 Kübler-Ross, *On Death and Dying*.

30 Plato, *The Republic*, London: Penguin Classics, 1970.

31 Matthew 18:10; Acts 12:15.
32 *Sunday Telegraph*, 19 December 1993.
33 Isaiah 6:2; Ephesians 3:10; Jude 9.
34 E. Swedenborg (1688–1772).
35 W. Blake (1757–1827).
36 R. Steiner (1861–1925), the founder of anthroposophy (a movement to develop the faculty of cognition and the realization of spiritual reality).
37 Gordon, *The Book of Miracles*.
38 R.H. Kirven, *Angels in Action*, Pennsylvania: Chrysalis, 1994.
39 Matthew 1:18–25; 2:13; Luke 1:26–38; 2:8–20.

CHAPTER FIVE

1 R. Pasco and J. Redford, *Faith Alive*, London: Hodder and Stoughton, 1988.
2 Luke 1:28.
3 Luke 1:42 (KJV).
4 Translated from the Roman Catholic Latin Bible.
5 Luke 16:28 (NEB).
6 Luke 23:43.
7 Genesis 4:1–16.
8 Exodus 20:1–17.
9 Deuteronomy 25:5–10.
10 Jung, *Memories, Dreams and Reflections*.
11 R. Sheldrake, *New Science of Life: The Hypothesis of Morphic Resonance*, Park Street, 1995.
12 I. Marshall.
13 Sheldrake, *New Science of Life*.
14 Marshall.
15 Jung, *Memories, Dreams and Reflections*.
16 1 Samuel 28:15 (KJV).
17 1 Kings 2:10 (NEB).
18 Daniel 12:2–3 (KJV).
19 Isaiah 26:19 (KJV).
20 J. Neuberger, in *My God*, ed. H. Mills and M. Maclaine, London: Pelham, 1988.
21 S. Brichto, in *My God*, ed. Mills and Maclaine.
22 W. Allen, Epigraph to Eric Lax, 1975.
23 J. Frazer, *The Golden Bough*, London: Macmillan, 1950.
24 'Go Forth, Christian Soul', *Pastoral Care of the Sick*, International Commission on English in the Liturgy, 1982.
25 J. Bowker, *The Complete Bible Handbook*, London: Dorling Kindersley, 1998.

26 Psalm 49:12, 14–15 (KJV).

27 Psalm 73:24–25 (KJV).

28 Ecclesiastes 7:1–4, 8 (NEB).

29 Ezekiel 37:1, 3–5 (KJV).

30 The Church of England Doctrine Commission, 1986.

31 Bowker, *The Complete Bible Handbook*.

32 Bowker, *The Complete Bible Handbook*.

33 G. Carey, *Millennium Message*, London: HarperCollins, 1999.

34 I. Paisley, in *My God*, ed. Mills and Maclaine.

35 A. Byrne, in *My God*, ed. Mills and Maclaine.

36 1 Corinthians 2:9.

37 G. Leonard, in *My God*, ed. Mills and Maclaine.

38 Mother Teresa, in *My God*, ed. Mills and Maclaine.

39 B. Graham, in *My God*, ed. Mills and Maclaine.

40 B. Kent, in *My God*, ed. Mills and Maclaine.

41 M. Muggeridge, in *My God*, ed. Mills and Maclaine.

42 R. Runcie, in *My God*, ed. Mills and Maclaine.

43 D. Soper, in *My God*, ed. Mills and Maclaine.

44 J. Polkinghorne, in *My God*, ed. Mills and Maclaine.

CHAPTER SIX

1 Ephesians 4:8–10.

2 John 11:38–44.

3 Matthew 19:16–22.

4 Romans 6:16, 22–23 (NEB).

5 Matthew 5:8 (KJV).

6 Matthew 6:9 (KJV).

7 Hebrews 4:9–10 (NEB).

8 Luke 16:19–31.

9 Matthew 16:19.

10 Quoted from a birthday card, Hanson White, 1994.

11 Matthew 12:32 (KJV).

12 1 Corinthians 3:13 (NEB).

13 1 Thessalonians 4:13–18 (NEB).

14 Revelation 14:1–3 (NEB).

15 Revelation 14:13 (NEB).

16 Matthew 25:31–33.

17 Luke 18:9–14.

18 Matthew 25:34–36 (NEB).

19 Matthew 25:40 (NEB).

20 Matthew 25:41 (NEB).

21 Revelation 20:10 (NEB).
22 Revelation 20:12–15 (NEB).
23 T. Grescoe, *Independent on Sunday Magazine*, 25 August 1996.
24 D. Bonhoeffer, *Letters and Papers from Prison*, London: SCM, 1981.
25 D. Byrne, 'Destiny Bay', in S. Stoddard, *The Hospice Movement*, London: Jonathan Cape, 1979.
26 Pope John XXIII.
27 John 14:3 (KJV).
28 Sister Carole, *Church of England Newspaper*, 21 November 1997.
29 John 14:19–20 (NEB).

Chapter Seven

1 D. Thomas, *The Poems*, London: J.M. Dent, 1974.
2 J. Diamond, journalist and broadcaster, has also been the subject of a television documentary on the subject of his cancer. His weekly column appeared in *The Times*.
3 From a letter to Valerie Grove, *The Times*.
4 From a letter to Valerie Grove, *The Times*.
5 *The Bill*, a police drama series, July 1999.
6 From a letter to the Society of Our Lady of the Isles from Mother Mary Agnes.
7 From a letter to the Society of Our Lady of the Isles from Mother Mary Agnes.
8 Quoted by Molly's mother to the author.
9 N. Cave, 'Into My Arms', Mute Song.
10 Plato, *The Apology*, Cambridge: Cambridge University, 1914.
11 R. Descartes, *A Discourse on Method*, Boston, Massachusetts: Tuttle, 1994.
12 M. Stroud, *Face to Face with Cancer*, Oxford: Lion, 1988.
13 D. Watson, *Fear No Evil*, London: Hodder and Stoughton, 1998.
14 Singh, *The Grace in Dying*.
15 Nuland, *How We Die*.
16 *The Craft of Dying*.
17 Stoddard, *The Hospice Movement*.
18 The Dalai Lama, *Kindness, Clarity and Insight*.
19 *The Tibetan Book of the Dead*.
20 J. Singer, in *The New Natural Death Handbook*, London: Rider, 1997.
21 D. Attwater, *Dictionary of Saints*, London: Penguin, 1965.

Chapter Eight

1 R.C. Fuller, *Crossing the Finishing Line: The Last Thoughts of Leonard Cheshire, v.c.*, London: St Pauls, 1998.

2 J. Jolliffe, *The Tablet*, 19 September 1998.
3 Matthew 6:34.
4 J. Davies, in *My God*, ed. Mills and Maclaine.
5 D. Alton, former Liberal Democrat MP and now a member of the House of Lords.
6 *The Guardian*, 26 May 1990.
7 Singh, *The Grace in Dying*.

CHAPTER NINE

1 Revelation 16:17–21.
2 M.A. Hai, *The Teachings of Islam*, Delhi: Mactaba Alhasanat, 1983.
3 D. Hathaway, *Prophetic Vision*, no. 12.
4 D. Thompson, *The End of Time*, London: Vintage, 1999.

CHAPTER TEN

1 H. Frazer, from a press cutting.
2 Frazer, from a press cutting.
3 Client survey by SCI.
4 *Church Times*, autumn 1998.
5 *Telegraph Magazine*, 17 October 1998.
6 R. Davey, from a press cutting.
7 *The Guardian*, 27 February 1996.
8 *Undercover Britain*, Channel Four.
9 J. Farrin, speaking at a study day on the British way of death at Westcott House, Cambridge, June 1999.
10 Farrin, speaking at a study day at Westcott House.
11 I. Alcock, from a press cutting.
12 G. Woodruffe, *Church Times*, 27 November 1998.
13 From the *Common Worship* funeral service, The Archbishops' Council, 2000.
14 Davies, *Death, Ritual and Belief*.
15 *Common Worship*.

CHAPTER ELEVEN

1 J. Tavener (b. 1944), 'Song for Athena'.
2 J. Seabrook, *Resurgence*, autumn 1997.
3 A.F. Cleese, *The Scotsman*, 11 August 1999.
4 Cleese, *The Scotsman*.
5 R. House, letter to *The Independent*, 1 September 1997.
6 N. Acherson, *Independent on Sunday*, 7 September 1997.

CHAPTER TWELVE

1 Sister Frances, from a press cutting.
2 D. Hay and R. Hay, *The Spirit of the Child*, London: HarperCollins, 1998.
3 Hay and Hay, *The Spirit of the Child*.
4 J. Hunter, 'Panic Attacks Late in Life and Change Before Life Ends',
   Psychoanalytic Psychotherapy, vol. 13, 1999.
5 N. Horlick, from a press cutting.
6 R. Crathorne, *UK Focus* March 1999.
7 Crathorne, *UK Focus*.

EPILOGUE

1 John 1:4 (KJV).
2 E. Kübler-Ross, *McCalls*, August 1976.
3 J. Marten-Meynell.
4 *The Fount Book of Prayer*, ed. R. Van de Weyer, London: HarperCollins,
   1993.
5 S. Daniel, sonnet 54, 'Delia', 1592.
6 T. Browne, *Religio Medici*, 1643.
7 'A Short Appreciation of this Exercise by Means of Question and Answer',
   ch. VI, *The Cloud of Unknowing*, fourteeth century.
8 L. Porter, Royal Corps of Signals (d. 1943, aged 31).
9 Luke 23:46 (KJV).

Acknowledgments

The English translation of 'Go Forth, Christian Soul', from *Pastoral Care of the Sick*, © 1982, International Committee on English in the Liturgy, Inc. All rights reserved.

Extracts from The Book of Common Prayer of 1662, the rights of which are vested in the Crown in perpetuity within the United Kingdom, are reproduced by permission of Cambridge University Press, Her Majesty's Printers.

Extracts from the *Common Worship* funeral service are copyright © The Archbishops' Council, 2000, and are reproduced by permission.

Extracts from the New English Bible, copyright © 1961, 1970, by Oxford University Press and Cambridge University Press.

Extracts from the Authorized Version of the Bible (The King James Bible), the rights in which are vested in the Crown, are reproduced by permission of the Crown's Patentee, Cambridge University Press.

Extract from 'Prayers in Time of Distress', from *Letters and Papers from Prison* by Dietrich Bonhoeffer, the Enlarged Edition, published by SCM Press, 1971.

Extract from 'Into My Arms' by Nick Cave, copyright © Mute Song, reproduced by permission.

Extract from 'Do Not Go Gentle into That Good Night', from *The Poems* by Dylan Thomas, published by J.M. Dent.

THE WAY OF HEALING
A collection of prayers and meditations from around
the world for all who seek healing and wholeness

Compiled by Lyn Klug

We all long for wholeness and healing – in our lives, in our
relationships and in the world around us. This fresh collection
of prayers and meditations embraces every form of healing, and
offers comfort, hope and encouragement for every stage of life.

As well as prayers for physical, mental and emotional well-
being, *The Way of Healing* includes prayers for the healing
of community, for the healing of grief and for forgiveness.
There are also helpful quotations for those seeking stillness
and harmony, for those praying for others and for those who
want to express their gratitude or compassion.

The book ends with a thoughtful selection of prayers written
by and for those who may be facing death.

ISBN 0 7459 4210 5 (hardback)

EXPERIENCES OF BEREAVEMENT

Helen Alexander

'The insights into what loving, living and dying are... leave
one silent with awe.'
Church Times

For all who are living through the shock and devastation of the
death of someone they love, this book shares experiences of grief,
offering comfort and strength. In a way that no textbook could
ever do, this book gives a unique understanding of the grief process
through the wide variety of experiences recounted. Whether the
reader is personally bereaved or supporting others, this powerful
book is essential reading.

ISBN 0 7459 3753 5 (paperback)